Climbing Higher

40 DEVOTIONS FOR HIKERS

LETTIE K. WHISMAN

Climbing Higher
40 DEVOTIONS
FOR HIKERS

LETTIE K. WHISMAN

Some Scriptures taken from the NEW INTERNATIONAL VERSION (NIV): Scripture taken from THE HOLY BIBLE, NEW INTERNATIONAL VERSION ®. Copyright© 1973, 1978, 1984, 2011 by Biblica, Inc.™. Used by permission of Zondervan

Scripture quotations identified NASB are from the New American Standard Bible, Copyright© by the Lockman Foundation.

Scripture quotations identified KJV are from the King James version.

All rights reserved. With the exception of brief quotations, no part of this publication may be reproduced, stored in a retrieval system, or transmitted in any form or by any means – electronic, mechanical, photocopying, recording, or otherwise – without the prior written permission of the copyright owner.

ISBN: 978-1-64288-259-9

Climbing Higher: 40 Devotions for Hikers
Copyright © 2022
Lettie Kirkpatrick Whisman
All Rights Reserved

Printed by Derek Press, Cleveland, TN

Cover by Wendy C. Brown

Dedication

Climbing Higher is dedicated to two influential forces in my undistinguished hiking career: The Cherokee Hiking Club and Linda Davis.

I became a member of the Cherokee Hiking Club in 2002. I was, at age 50, a novice hiker, but eager to learn and experience outdoor adventures. Despite coming late to the trails, I was welcomed and built many friendships. The seeds of this book were actually planted, walking paths with these folks.

The Cherokee Hiking Club:

- Educated me about plants, flowers, trees, trail locations, trail safety and equipment. It is an endless list.
- Encouraged me. They were eager to see other folks as enthusiastic about hiking as they were. Hiking brings a contagious joy.
- Enlarged my coasts. This term from 1 Chronicles 4:10, certainly applies to what I have received from the hiking community as they have stretched me to experience new adventures and push my limits.
- Endured with me. In 2012, my hiking days were abruptly halted as I cared for my husband following a massive stroke. But despite our limitations, my club showed up so many times in so many ways during the next five years. They did not forget us.

One special hiking club member that took me "under her wings" was Linda Davis. Linda patiently taught me to canoe. In my early club days, we worked on a trail construction together and just discussed life. But cancer claimed Linda's life before my caregiving days began. I have included one of her story donations in *Climbing Higher*. And our club still does an annual walk in her memory.

I know Linda's spunky challenge and prayer would be for all of us to take to the trails and let God "enlarge our coasts" indeed!

And Jabez called on the God of Israel, saying, Oh that thou wouldest bless me indeed, and enlarge my coast. (1 Corinthians 4:10 KJV)

Linda Davis
9/20/1953 - 6/17/2008

Contents

Acknowledgements..9
Foreword from Tazz Reid..10
Preface..11

Section One – Trail Legends

1. Never Say Old..15
2. Music on the Mountains..................................17
3. Sight . . . Unseen 19
4. Grandma Hikes, Too!.......................................21
5. Two Forty-Year Hikes 23
6. Intrigued by Trees 24
7. Nine Days 25

Section Two – Trail Treasures

8. Eclipsed 31
9. Glorious Epiphany 33
10. Coming Together 35
11. New!..37
12. More Than a Stick 39
13. Fire 41
14. I Once Was Lost...43
15. Miracles On the Trail 45
16. Nature Speaks...49
17. Sharing The Joy...53

Hooked On Hiking

Section Three – Trail Adventures

18. Here Hikes the Bride 59

Contents..*continued*

19. A "Lucky" Miracle?...61
20. Chasing a Dream 63
21. Two Joshuas 65
22. Bug Eaters 67
23. Sleeping With a Bear 69
24. Pick Your Guide...71
25. Heroes 73
26. Wild No More 75
27. No Hiker Left Behind..77
28. Trails, Toilets, and Happy Endings..........................79

Section Four – Trail Lessons

29. Breaking the Rules 83
30. Decisions, Decisions! 85
31. Learning the Hard Way 87
32. Traveling Light?..89
33. Trail Tragedies 91
34. Along the Way 93
35. A Helping Hand 95
36. Huffy Breaths and Bear Cubs 97
37. A Perfect Day for Sand Flies 99
38. Waiting for Spring...101
39. A Parable of the Saunterer 105
40. Hike's End..107

About the Author 109

Acknowledgements

I am tremendously indebted to the giftedness, skills, and willingness of "the team" that helped this book happen.

- Wendy Brown who patiently persevered (I am so limited in decision making skills!) in creating the perfect cover for *Climbing Higher*. She did this in the middle of her own health care crisis.

- Rita Ross who catches my vision and creates the final product after disrupting her own life and responsibilities. This is our fourth book together. And we are still friends!

- The unseen prayer warriors and friends that surround and carry me in every book project. Theirs is the heavy work that accomplishes God's good work.

- My patient, encouraging husband. Jim's wife mostly disappears during book construction.

- Last, the incredible and generous gift of Tazz Reid and Susan Holmes in not only giving me access to *Weekly Word Outdoor Adventures* as a resource for this book but are offering it as a companion to their weekly Facebook production.

Foreword

My social media account had been dormant for several years, and the church account wasn't much better. And then the pandemic hit! Suddenly social media became very important to churches everywhere, and Cleveland Community Chapel not only began posting each of our three services, but we also started a new outdoor ministry called *The Weekly Word Outdoor Adventures*. It was to be about finding God in His marvelous creation. I modeled it loosely after Bill Landry's "The Heartland Series" about people, places and things in Appalachia. Only I gave it a religious twist.

I knew who Lettie Kirkpatrick Whisman was from bumping into her, in town, from time to time, and we had mutual friends, who had informed me that she was a dear sister in Christ. Then one day she called and made an appointment to come by my office. Lettie had become a watcher of *The Weekly Word Outdoor Adventures*, and she explained to me how much earlier, before the pandemic, she had started, in print, something along the same theme of experiencing God in the outdoors. It was basically the same thing we were doing with video. Lettie asked if she could use some of my ideas. After discussing it with my camera/ technology person, Susan Holmes, our mutual reply was, "Anything we have produced and put out there is for the glory of God, and it belongs to the kingdom". We were delighted to be asked for its use.

Lettie had left with me some of her books that were previously published. It was in reading those that I got to know her heart. Lettie is someone who, through the Refiner's fires of suffering, has grown into a tremendous woman of God. In the following pages you will find she has skillfully interwoven Biblical teaching with outdoor experiences. *Tazz Reid*

Tazz is the Pastor of Cleveland Community Chapel and the Creator and Narrator of Weekly Word Outdoor Adventures.

Preface

The seed, or vision, if you will, for this book came as I was emerging from one of the darkest seasons of my life. When my husband of 29 years died of cancer, I thought for a while that my future had died with him. Hope was a foreign word, although, thank God, my friends held to it for me.

Always a walker, I found myself longing for the mountains and their solitary trails. It was as I began hiking, I discovered reprieve from the sadness. I also found a new companionship with my awesome Creator God. As I hiked, often just Him and me, I came to understand that I would survive even this. One might say that hope returned.

One of my sons referred to my frequent wooded ramblings as "wandering." It was with great delight I one day discovered Psalm 56:8-9: "Thou hast taken account of my wanderings. Put my tears in Thy bottle. Are they not in thy book? . . . This I know that God is for me."

Scottish Olympic runner Eric Liddell is reported to have said, "When I run, I feel God's pleasure." I understand. It is there when I hike. Because I know the God of creation, I worship and pay homage as I observe His handiwork.

The Psalmist said that God gave him "songs in the night," God truly did give me this book topic in the night. I had never seen a book of devotions for hikers. It was exciting to me, the idea of combining two of my passions into a tool for drawing hearts to the trails and to the God of the trails.

I began compiling this book with great excitement and loved pulling together hiking stories from friends, books, historical hiking heroes, and news clippings. I could not have known nearly 10 years would pass as I cared for and buried yet another husband. It was a season that made me doubtful I would ever write again. But my desire to complete this book never disappeared. Finally, I knew it must happen. And, with God's help, it truly has.

I offer you *Climbing Higher*.

Lettie Kirkpatrick Whisman

> *If the trails could talk*
> *If the woods could speak*
> *If the mountains could bring forth the glad tidings that John Muir welcomed . . .*
> *We would have stories pour forth and they would tell of laughter and tears and joy and friendship.*
> *They would speak of lost boys and weddings, of courage, strength, healing, and incredible adventures . . . of breathtaking beauty and God encounters that changed lives.*
> *Let the stories speak*

Trail Legends

Climbing Higher

"Man has created some lovely dwellings – some soul stirring literature. He has done much to alleviate physical pain. But he has not . . . created a substitute for a sunset, a grove of pines, the music of the winds, the dank smell of the deep forest or the shy beauty of the wildflowers."
(Harvey Broome, Naturalist)

"It were as well to be educated in the shadow of a mountain as in more classic shade. Some will remember no doubt not only that they went to college, but that they went to the mountain."
(Henry David Thoreau)

Photo Credit: Jason Beck
AT Thru-Hiker, 2021

1

Never Say Old

Even when I am old and gray, do not forsake me,
O God, till I declare your power to the next generation,
your might to all who are to come
(Psalms 71:18 NIV)

Grace (Gracie) McNicol had a late-in-life love affair. But it wasn't with a man. It was with Mount Le Conte, a 6,500-foot mountain in the Great Smoky Mountains National Park. Accessible only by footpath, five trails lead to the lodge where hikers receive a hot meal and sleeping quarters, as well as an amazing view.

Gracie began climbing Mount Le Conte at age 62. That was her age when she retired from nursing in Alaska and moved to Maryville, Tennessee, where she continued working as a nurse. Her last climb was on September 30, 1983, the day she arrived on horseback in celebration of her 92nd birthday! She climbed the mountain a total of 244 times, 155 by foot and 89 by horseback as she became less agile.

Charles Kuralt had Gracie interviewed for his radio program *Exploring America*, and later described her as the "90-year-old girl" and "one tireless American, tireless in pursuit of her dreams." Climbing this mountain regularly was the dream she pursued. The biography of Gracie's love affair with Le Conte, *Gracie and the Mountain*, indicates "those who knew her best say that Gracie 'grew young' trekking up Mount LeConte."

Shortly before her death at age 100, Gracie told a friend, "I'm climbing Mount LeConte in my mind this year. I can almost see the red bee balm and turtleheads blooming beside the Bullhead

Climbing Higher

Trail." In explaining her passion for Le Conte and her persistence in returning so frequently to "her mountain," Gracie acknowledged, "I feel closest to God on Mount Le Conte when I am among all the splendor He has created for us to enjoy . . . from the tiniest spring beauty flower to the mountain itself and all the stars in the heavens above."

We often see the phrase "the graying of America," referring to our aging population. Our culture seems to have a fixation on youth, often ignoring the wealth of wisdom and skill seniors have to contribute. Gracie's life was a reminder and inspiration that there is much to be embraced even in this season of life.

In the Bible, some of the greatest victories were realized by God's aging servants. Moses received his assignment from God at age 80. Abraham welcomed his promised heir at 100. Caleb took the land of his inheritance at 85.

Even the last years of our journey can be filled with joy. And anticipation of eternity where we will truly realize "pleasures forevermore."

HIKING QUOTE:
"In the woods, too, a man casts off his years . . .
In the woods is perpetual youth. . .
In the woods we return to reason and faith."
(Ralph Waldo Emerson, U.S. essayist, 1803-1882)

HIKING TRIVIA: Gracie competed with an Episcopal priest, Rufus Morgan, for the title of "most trips up Le Conte." They both climbed the mountain at age 92.

2

Music on the Mountains

*Let the rivers clap their hands,
let the mountains sing together for joy
(Psalm 98:8 NIV)*

July 15, 2005 was a day of celebration. It was the grand opening day hike of the Benton MacKaye Trail from Mud Gap to Whigg Meadow. Over 100 people attended the opening ceremony of the newest long-distance trail in the country. One group would hike north to Beech Gap, while a second group would walk south to Whigg Meadow.

Then an unanticipated occurrence brought an unforgettable flavor to the occasion. Four members of a Korean hiking club in Atlanta had learned of the event and came to join the gathering. As they participated in the hike, one of them mentioned that the Korean National Anthem also spoke of majestic mountains.

As a result of this conversation, a request was made that they sing their national anthem. They replied they would rather hear the American anthem as they now considered themselves Americans. Their fellow hikers obliged as the Korean guests joined them. They then followed with the Korean National Anthem.

An account was later given of this event on the Benton MacKaye website. George Owen wrote, "It was the singing of both the Korean and American National Anthems with a crowd of people standing in the cloud on Whigg Meadow. Then someone suggested "America the Beautiful." Then it was proposed we sing "This Land is Your Land," which we did. By that time, I confess I was getting a little misty-eyed by it all. It was just a wonderful spontaneous moment that made a magnificent hike even greater. Unforgettable."

Psalm 100 tells us that we are to come into God's presence with thanksgiving and into His courts with praise. There is perhaps, no better way to praise God than with song, even for those making a joyful "noise" to the Lord. And there is nothing that better promotes praise, especially spontaneous praise, than to be standing amidst His marvelous creation, knowing the reality of Hebrews 11:3 that "the worlds were framed by the word of God."

How pleased He must have been with the explosion of praise on Whigg Meadow as both Korean and American hikers followed the admonition in Psalm 105: 2 to "sing praise to Him."!

Story Credit: Linda Davis, who was an avid hiker and a member of the Benton Mackaye Hiking Club, the Hiwassee and Cherokee Hiking Club and the National Hiking Society.

HIKING QUOTE: "Many people, after a few days in the wilderness (sometimes after only a few hours) feel themselves to be more themselves, uncluttered and spontaneous." (Eugene Peterson)

3

Sight . . . Unseen

*But He knows the way I take;
When He has tried me,
I shall come forth as gold.
My foot has held fast to His path
(Job 23:10-ll NASB)*

Long Distance Hiker, Ed Talone, would tell anyone that Sue Lockwood was one of the most amazing hikers he's ever known. And he should know. After meeting her in 1992, he hiked alongside of her on many trails, including the North Country Trail. They are two of only a handful of hikers that have actually completed this 4,400-mile trail.

But, what was so amazing about Sue? Besides the fact that the former teacher and basketball coach while battling diabetes, continued hiking 20,000 plus miles even after the loss of her sight and her kidneys? Could it be her tenacity as she was forced to complete each hiking section so she could return daily to her brother's van for dialysis? Or would it be the spunk that kept her moving, along with her guide dog (and often Ed), for hike after hike?

Ed remembers a particularly poignant event from one hike with Sue. It occurred when they were on an Ohio section of the North Country Trail. Darkness came as they were on an overgrown section of the trail, and they could not continue forward. They decided to retrace their steps and return the way they came. But the flashlight batteries soon gave out and Ed found himself searching for the trail with only the moonlight to guide him.

Climbing Higher

To Ed's amazement, Sue suddenly informed him, "You are 20 yards too high." Ed followed her suggested direction and found the trail – at a place where a previous trail actually intersected the current trail! They were able to follow it out, but it remains a mystery how Sue's sightless eyes so accurately directed Ed's search.

Sometimes we may wonder if God truly "knows" where we are. Does He see our suffering, our weariness, our discouragement? Does He know about our doubts? In Genesis 16, Hagar, a pregnant, rejected servant, declares, after an encounter with the Lord, "Thou art a God who sees." The Psalmist wrote, "Even the darkness is light to Him."

A pastor once indicated that people in pain do not so much need to know if God is there. Their question is, "Does God care?" Yes to both questions. He is there and He does care.

HIKING QUOTE: "I have never been lost, but I will admit to being confused for a few weeks." (Daniel Boone, *The Great Bushwhacker*)

HIKING TRIVIA: Sue was blessed with a remarkable caregiver. Her brother, Gordon Smith, served as her "hiker's helper," bringing her portable dialysis machine from trail to trail to allow her to continue her pursuit of hiking.

4

Grandma Hikes, Too!

*Even to your old age and gray hair I am he,
I am he who will sustain you.
(Isaiah 46:4 NIV)*

Hulda Crooks is a legend to regular climbers of Mount Whitney, which is part of the Sierra Nevada mountain range in eastern California. She is said to have climbed the 14,505-foot peak, the highest in the continental U.S., at least 23 times. She accomplished those climbs between the ages of 65 and 91, during which time she also climbed 97 other peaks. She became known as "Grandma Whitney" and even had a nearby peak renamed in her honor.

Born in 1896 and raised on a Canadian Farm, Hulda began serious climbing in her 60s. At 91 she added Mt. Fiji in Japan to her hikes accomplished and also hiked the 212-mile John Muir Trail. Hulda died in 1997 at age 101. A small park in Loma Linda is named in her honor. It contains a bronze statue of the 90-year-old with a broad hat and a hiking stick.

Another hiking grandma, born a few years before Hulda Crooks, was Emma Gatewood, best known for her hikes on the 2,190-mile Appalachian Trail. The Ohio native also got a late start, completing the trail in 146 days on her second attempt at age 67. The first woman to solo hike the AT, she was the mother of 11, grandmother of 23, and the survivor of years of domestic abuse. Emma hiked in canvas tennis shoes, used a shower curtain for a tarp, and carried a handsewn knapsack filled with fruit, Vienna sausage and nuts. In 1964 at age 76, Emma Gatewood hiked the trail a third time.

Climbing Higher

These women were remarkable senior adults. They remind us of the importance of reaching for high goals at any age. The Bible actually includes stories of several noteworthy seniors and their accomplishments as well.

- *Abraham's wife, Sarah, gave birth and was raising a newborn son in her nineties! (Genesis 21)*
- *Caleb, one of the last survivors of the Israelites 40-year camping trip, subdued and defeated enemy tribes at age 85 so he could inherit his land (a mountain) and build a city in Judah. (Joshua 14)*
- *We know that another set of elderly parents, Elizabeth and Zechariah, "well advanced in age" were raising John the Baptist in the wilderness while Anna (in her 80s) was in the temple announcing that the Messiah had been born. (Luke Chapters 1 and 2)*

Although our nation promotes a culture of retirement in the sixth and seventh decades, perhaps we need to reconsider. It might just be the perfect time to climb some mountains, hike some trails, or even break some personal records. Or to find opportunity to make a difference in the world and lives around us.

> HIKING QUOTE: "I dream of hiking into my old age. I want to be able, even then, to pack my load and take off slowly, but steadily along the trail." (Marilyn Doan, *Hiking Light*)

5

Two Forty-Year Hikes

*Then Moses climbed Mount Nebo
from the plains of Moab
to the top of Pisgah,
across from Jericho.
(Deuteronomy 34:1 NIV)*

Some folks prefer to hike alone. Others believe there is more fun (and safety) in numbers. Some are happy either way.

But in 1852, a legend began when a man named Mason Kershaw Evans took to the mountains and stayed there until his death 40 years later. At the time of his flight to the forest, Mason was prominent in his community as a militia leader and a schoolteacher. He was raised in the Starr Mountain area, which is part of the Cherokee National Forest and extends through Polk, McMinn, and Monroe counties in Tennessee. He was no stranger to the woods that became his home.

It is speculated that the trauma of a romantic rejection led to a mental breakdown and his subsequent decision to spend the remainder of his life in the solitary lodging of Panther Cave on Starr Mountain. His choice of living quarters led to his designation as the Starr Mountain Hermit, only one of the colorful phrases used to describe Mason Evans.

The years of his mountain wanderings included the Civil War. It is quite conceivable that he observed much of the coming and going of the soldiers from the vantage point of his mountain cave and nearby bluffs. Locals often provided necessities for him and seemed to look the other way when he helped himself to their garden produce and even their chickens. A nearby resort

Climbing Higher

hotel owner is believed to have fed him often. For some years his family lived close by as well and contributed clothes and food.

But Evans eventually died alone in his late 60s, still hiking the mountains that became his hiding place from a world he had long left behind. His body was found in January 1892.

*The Bible tells of a prominent character who also experienced a 40-year wilderness "retreat." Only Moses, who may have often wished he **was** alone, was babysitting, at God's direction, a nation of grumpy and immature Israelites that he had rescued from Egyptian slavery (an estimated 600,000 of them!). While Mason was blessed with community assistance, Exodus 16 tells us the provision for these folks came directly from God (quail and manna straight from heaven) and their clothing and shoes, miraculously, never wore out (Deuteronomy 29:5). Like Mason, Moses was also familiar with mountains. God gave him the Ten Commandments on Mount Sinai. And before his death, God led him to a place called Mount Nebo in the land of Moab. It was there, God allowed him to see the land that would become the home of the Jewish nation. While the body of Mason was found and given burial, we are told in Deuteronomy 34 that God Himself buried His servant Moses in Moab in a location known only to Him.*

Book Credit:
Torment in the Knobs
(Frank McKinney)

Story Credit: Weekly Word Outdoor Adventures (Tazz Reid/Susan Holmes)

6
Intrigued by Trees

*The Lord God made all kinds of trees grow out of the ground –
trees that were pleasing to the eye and good for food
(Genesis 2:9 NIV)*

"I think that I shall never see a poem lovely as a tree."
(Joyce Kilmer)

Some trails lead to a destination – a waterfall, a landmark, spectacular views, a completed accomplishment. Sometimes the trail itself is the goal. That would be the case in the Joyce Kilmer Memorial Forest. In 1936, the 3,800-acre forest was named after the author of the poem "Trees." Joyce Kilmer was killed in action in World War I. The forest is located near Robbinsville, North Carolina, on the Cherohala Skyway. It contains about 100 tree species, including sycamore, hemlock, oak, and yellow poplar. Some are over 400 years old, more than 20 feet in circumference and 100 feet tall.

The best views of the trees are found by hiking a two-mile loop trail. With the hemlock blight and weather erosion, recent years have taken a toll on the trail. But the forest, the trail and the spectacular trees remain on the must-see list for many hikers.

Interestingly enough, the Bible begins and ends with the presence of trees. Genesis 2 speaks of two specific trees: The tree of life and the tree of the knowledge of good and evil. God issued a rule regarding the second tree and the breaking of it brought great consequences for all mankind. But in Acts 5:30, we see God's mercy/remedy for the rebellious nature that still plagues us – it was to send Jesus to hang on a "tree," the cross that provides the bridge back to God. And then in Revelation 2:7, the tree of life reappears in a new location.

Climbing Higher

However, in between fulfillment of God's divine plan, we continue to see the role of trees in "His" story. One particular tree shows up several times. A broom tree or juniper, considered a short desert shrub, may be the one used to shade Ishmael in Genesis 21 when his mother Hagar is abandoned. Elijah found shelter under this small tree while he fled from Jezebel and experienced God's care as he rested (I Kings 19:4). Job referred to the roots of the tree as a source of food for the desperate (Job 30:3-4). And, of course, the sycamore tree gained fame in Luke 19 as the ladder provided for Zacchaeus to observe Jesus as he journeyed to faith.

Many of us have our own tree stories. A small, gnarled tree on our property is referred to as "The Gideon Tree" because my young grandson, Gideon, discovered the branches were a perfect fit for his little legs to climb.

Who could deny the truth of Joyce Kilmer's final conclusion in his poem Trees. "Poems are made by fools like me, but only God can make a tree." Yes Indeed!

Story Credit: *Weekly Word Outdoor Adventures* (Tazz Reid/Susan Holmes)

HIKING QUOTE: "If people in general could be got into the woods, even for once, to hear the trees speak for themselves, all difficulties in the way of forest preservation would vanish." (John Muir)

7

Nine Days

*See that you do not despise one of these little ones.
For I tell you that their angels in heaven
always see the face of my Father in heaven.
(Matthew 18:10 NIV)*

Twelve-year-old Donn Fendler from Rye, New York could have never imagined that his Boy Scout training and his personal courage would provide his means of survival during nine days alone in the wilderness of Maine's Mount Katahdin Forest. His own story account is told in the book *LOST on a Mountain in Maine*. The book's forward indicates, "this slight, highly nervous, city-bred child survived nine heartbreaking days in a wilderness . . . that would overwhelmingly test the strength of the most experienced backwoods guide."

Donn's "extraordinary" adventure began July 17, 1939. He left a campsite at Katahdin Stream with his faifther, two brothers, and two friends to take a climb up Hunt Trail. When Donn and his friend Henry pulled away from the group on the chilly, cloud covered mountain, Donn's attempt to return set in motion the chain of events that would captivate millions and create a lasting legend.

Donn's story is a gripping account of a young boy's incredible perseverance and endurance. He spent nine days lost, often sleeping in tree stumps, subsisting on berries and water, surviving a fall from a rock, trekking shoeless mile after mile through underbrush, brutal rugged terrain and fighting for his sanity. Simple scout rules like "keep your head" and "when lost, follow a stream down" became powerful survival tools. He later spoke of his daily prayers and the sense that "someone" seemed

Climbing Higher

to be with him and wanted him to "get out of those woods and go home."

Forest creatures like bear, deer, and chipmunk penetrated his solitude and provided mental distraction. Donn endured the physical torment of endless mosquito bites and attacks of blackflies, moose flies, and copperhead flies. Horrific foot wounds and injuries resulted from his barefoot journey.

Although 400-500 searchers included the National Guard, Forestry Service, Maine State Police and firefighters, timber cruisers, and blood hounds, the search was eventually considered futile, and speculation was that only a body would be found. His actual survival as he stumbled onto open water and, close by, an occupied cabin, was predicted by no one.

One would be hard pressed to convince Donn Fendler that his miraculous survival wasn't just that --- miraculous. The book forward indicates Donn spoke with certainty that a guardian angel not only guided, but "pulled" him along. The Bible, of course, provides numerous accounts of angels stepping briefly into the affairs of men. Very often their first remarks are "don't be afraid." God himself gives us that same admonition multiple times in Scripture. No wonder Donn indicates one of his great comforts and motivations as he pushed through the woods was the sense that he wasn't alone.

STORY TRIVIA: Donn Findley died in 2016 at age 90. He acquired the rank of Life Scout and spent years sharing his story with school children. As an adult, he revisited the path of his incredible wilderness trek. Donn also experienced a military career that included serving with special forces in Vietnam.

DONN FENDLER

Lost on A Mountain in Maine

Trail Treasures

Climbing Higher

"John Calvin occasionally pointed out that one of the reasons God created human beings to stand upright is precisely so we can lift our gaze to the Heavens, praising God for the celestial wonders we see in the night sky."
(Scott Hoezze, Remember Creation)

Photo Credit: Brian A. Boyd
Tallulah Falls, Georgia
August 21, 2017

8

Eclipsed!

The heavens declare the glory of God;
the skies proclaim the work of his hands
(Psalm 19:1 NIV)

August 21, 2017 truly was a wondrous day. It was preceded by days of excitement around the world as anticipation built for the coming eclipse. Motels were full and traffic was heavy as travelers pushed to be in locations of greatest visibility. Even the lakes and rivers were filled with boats attempting to bypass crowds on the highways.

The Cherokee Hiking Club gathered in the east Tennessee mountain home of Richard and Brenda Harris. They were perfectly located in the "band of totality" to experience the long-awaited eclipse. Club members drove winding rural roads to access the Harris cabin which was nestled between the woods and a clearing, perfectly located for observation of this incredible event. Thousands had gathered elsewhere in these same mountains to view a spectacle that would only last a few minutes.

The momentum built as club members chatted, donned eclipse glasses and viewed the gradual, then total entry into darkness. It was amazing. The air cooled, dogs began howling, and even lightning bugs emerged! Observers were left breathless and awestruck. There was an undeniable awareness of what the Bible refers to as God's revelation through creation.

As folks flooded out of the mountains to make their way home, visitors from many states became partners in awe as they chatted in the afterglow of God's glory in the heavens and His work in

Climbing Higher

the earth below. It was a moment when God's display of power briefly united a deeply divided humanity.

Pursue a moment to remember God as creator. Watch as the sun sets, sit still before a star filled sky, or take a walk along a quiet trail in the woods or beside a creek. Worship the One who spoke our world into existence and even knows the stars by name (Isaiah 40:26).

"When I top Bob's Bald, or Whigg Meadow, or the Hangover, or any mountain vista .... be it Glacier, Tetons, Grand Canyon, the song, 'How Great Thou Art,' always comes to mind." (Brenda Harris, Cherokee Hiking Club – Lyrics by Carl Boberg)

> O LORD my God when I in awesome wonder
> Consider all the works Thy hand hath made,
> I see the stars, I hear the mighty thunder,
> Thy power throughout the universe displayed;
>
> When through the woods and forest glades I wander
> And hear the birds sing sweetly in the trees;
> When I look down from lofty mountain grandeur,
> And hear the brook, and feel the gentle breeze;
>
> Then sings my soul, my Saviour God, to thee,
> How great Thou art! How great Thou art!
> Then sings my soul, my Saviour God, to thee,
> How great Thou art! How great Thou art!

9

Glorious Epiphany

*He giveth snow like wool:
he scattereth the hoarfrost like ashes.
(Psalm 147:16 KJV)*

I had decided to brave the cold with my good friend for a hike at Fort Mountain State Park in north Georgia. After all, December birthdays should be celebrated even though it was a sad season for me as a new widow.

Elizabeth and I bundled up for the 28-degree weather and headed up the mountain. But nothing could have prepared us for the birthday surprise that was coming.

As the elevation increased, we rounded the corner to discover a spectacular sight. Everywhere we looked the branches and bushes were decorated with the most incredible layers of white – not exactly snow, not exactly ice, but delicate crystals overwhelming the landscape.

We stood breathless in wonder and baffled at the indescribable beauty. What were we witnessing? As we parked and approached a ranger, he explained we had encountered a phenomenon called hoarfrost. During the night a cloud had descended on the mountain which would ordinarily result in fog. Instead, the condensation had frozen and produced the scene before us.

We walked from trail to trail and around the lake in awestruck sighing. I was certain that I was receiving a birthday gift I would never forget. It was a moment when heaven touched earth and I understood, even in my loss, I truly mattered. Look what God had prepared for his grieving daughter!

Climbing Higher

In the book **Captivating** *by John and Stasi Eldredge, Stasi describes her own epiphany. Taking an ocean walk, she had asked God to meet her in nature in a very specific way. It soon became apparent her request would not be granted. Instead, she walked onto a path of beach and into her own breathless wonder – multitudes of starfish all shapes, sizes, and colors! She wrote of the encounter with God's unique and personal surprise using words like "extravagant abundance," "heart explosion," and "an intimate gift from an intimate God."*

After my hoarfrost experience, I understand this. So would the reader of **Captivating** *who asked God for her own starfish and received instead an incredible wildflower field bursting with white lilies, orange poppies, purple and yellow wildflowers.*

Hikers would also get it. God's word indicates that "He takes pleasure in His people" (Psalm 149:4) and "Delights to give us the kingdom" (Luke 12:32). We might also add He pours out on us – hoarfrost, starfish, wildflowers, and anything else in creation that brings us joyful laughter and heart explosions. What have been your own glorious epiphanies?

10

Coming Together

*In the future when your descendants ask their parents,
"What do these stones mean?" tell them,
"Israel crossed the Jordan on dry ground"
(Joshua 4:21-22 NIV)*

It used to be for guys only – the twice-yearly camping trip established by the Kirkpatrick family. However, the expedition to the wild mushroomed over time to include the entire clan, which consisted of parents, five adult children with spouses, numerous grandchildren, and any friends lucky enough to receive an invite.

The "real" outdoorsmen of the group considered the trip a highlight of the year. Those less inclined toward roughing it enjoyed the outing because it brought together family members whose busy schedules normally took them in numerous diverse directions.

Camping originally took place in tents beside a roaring creek in a totally uncivilized (as in no toilets) location. But the clan patriarch and matriarch were eventually allowed the luxury of a pop-up camper that was eyed with envy by several previously gung-ho survivalists. Camp menu now included a huge breakfast and later an evening cookout.

The evening cookout preceded an established tradition which children awaited with suspenseful anticipation – the telling of exciting stories around the campfire, accompanied by visual and sound effects with each year's narrative intended to outdo the previous one. This event is recounted with great relish in the following months.

Climbing Higher

Of course, hiking, fishing, and occasionally wading completed weekend activities. Each year a group photo records the addition of cousins, as well as the changes (as in aging and size) of family and friends

This family event brings to mind a unique camping trip in the Bible that also spanned the generations. It was a 40-year journey beginning with the parting of the Red Sea and requiring years of dependence on God's protection and provision. In Joshua, chapters 3 and 4, God instructed Joshua to pick up stones from the Jordan River as He parted yet another body of water and they crossed over on dry land. They were to set the stones up on the other side. The purpose of the rock formation was to remind the Israelite family of God's great works among them and to prepare a visual to be used to tell their children and grandchildren of His faithfulness.

The annual camping trips introduced a real sense of cohesiveness into the Kirkpatrick family unit. The children attending received a fresh awareness of continuity and created wonderful memories. Like the legacy provided by these two "family" camping trips, we need to be sharing our stories of God's faithfulness and presence with the people God places in our lives.

11

New!

See, I am doing a new thing!
Now it springs up . . .
I am making a way in the wilderness
and streams in the wasteland.
(Isaiah 43:19 NIV)

The vision was birthed at a hiking conference in 2001. It was the vision for a new trail to be called the Great Eastern Trail. It would be a path of about 1,700 miles connecting a network of already existing trails and linking the Florida-Alabama line to New York's Finger Lakes.

The trail would be constructed primarily on public lands (some trail groups would need to purchase or negotiate donations of land) and, with some direction provided by the American Hiking Society, would rely solely on volunteers to craft and connect the trails together. When completed, the Great Eastern Trail would stretch west of the Appalachian Trail, providing an alternative to this much used and often abused trail.

Beginning in Alabama's, the Great Eastern Trail will meander through forests, climb cliff tops, and wander down logging trails as it stretches from Georgia to Tennessee and past Chattanooga through caves and overlooks on into Virginia, Kentucky, West Virginia, Maryland, and Pennsylvania before it ends across the New York border.

As of 2022, the Great Eastern Trail is still under development. But it is considered 70 percent completed. Updates are available at www.greateasterntrail.org.

Climbing Higher

It is exciting to participate in something with the word "new" attached. A new home, a new baby, a new school – "new" conveys a fresh start, a completed vision, or a beginning adventure.

What about the possibility that we can have a new beginning as a new person with our lives redeemed from bad choices, personal scars, and past failures? A new beginning that can be accompanied by power to change, that brings the promise of a purpose-full life followed by eternal life with God? God can give us that. Hope is offered in 2 Corinthians 5:17 to anyone who follows Christ. The promise? "Therefore, if anyone is in Christ, the new creation has come: The old has gone, the new is here."

TRAIL TRIVIA: One of the volunteer trail builders and a former nuclear engineer, Warren Devine, referred to one of the staircases on a Soddy Daisy, Tennessee, portion of the Great Eastern Trail: "It's going to be there longer than all the paperwork I grind out. The staircase down there is going to last a century."

12

More Than a Stick

For thou art with me; thy rod and thy staff they comfort me.
(Psalm 23:4 KJV)

A very high percentage of folks "trekking" a trail, carry a hiking stick of some kind, at least those who regularly and seriously explore the outdoors. But there are some who disdain their use as unnecessary and even more of a liability than an asset. And, of course, there is debate about which has the greater value – a plain wood hiking stick or the more sophisticated trekking poles.

Many hikers can attest to a time they have been rescued from a fall by the balancing factor of their stick. And most would acknowledge a multitude of different purposes that have been served by their trusty poles. Besides the fall prevention factor, there are other additional benefits:

1. The path clearing value of a stick is undeniable. Early morning cobwebs, large and impressive spiderwebs (especially those containing spiders!), and trail debris can be easily pushed aside with the use of a pole. But even more memorable for most is the value of scooting aside a lethargic snake, or in the event of a refusal to budge, simply lifting them away and off the trail.

2. Physically, pole advocates indicate they offer multiple aid. There is the assistance with balance, better distribution of body weight, and a reduction of stress on back, knees, legs, and feet. Just carrying a stick is also believed to burn more calories as well as allow for increased speed and extra endurance.

Climbing Higher

3. Hiking sticks are a huge help while crossing the rocks and wet wood of creeks and streams. They not only assess depth and the stability of the footpath but can probe ahead of boots to determine the next best step.

4. Then there are the bragging rights that come when a hiking stick is used as a "trophy" holder. It becomes an interesting conversation piece when filled with clamp-on medallions that tell the story of adventures lived and trails conquered.

Perhaps one of the most fun uses of a hiking stick was by the blind hiker Sue Lockwood (see the devotion "Sight Unseen"). Ed Talone remembers her habit of cheerfully using her stick to draw the word "Hi!" on the path – leaving the mark of her presence for those coming after her.

The Psalmist (in this case King David), when referencing God's rod, also found positive purposes. In Psalm 23, also known as the Shepherd's Psalm, he saw it to be a reminder of God's presence and direction.

Just as hikers determine the purpose and use of their stick, the shepherd can use his rod to bring guidance, protection, or even discipline to his flock. It symbolizes his position of authority and responsibility toward them.

Although the stick of a hiker is certainly a practical tool, perhaps the visual it provides of the shepherd's rod can also be a sweet reminder of our own Good Shepherd and His care.

13

Fire!

*When you walk through the fire, you will not be burned;
the flames will not set you ablaze (Isaiah 43:2 NIV)*

Tazz Reid walked through the charred wooded area on Starr Mountain in the Cherokee National Forest. He explained to his viewers on the *Weekly Word Outdoor Adventures* program that this prescribed burn which appeared so destructive, actually held multiple benefits for the outdoor community. Hunters eventually would discover an increase in wildlife such as turkey and deer. They would be attracted to this area because they could move more freely into the open space that now had less dense ground cover. Animals and hikers would enjoy discovering the new plant life springing up to renew the scorched earth. What had appeared to be deliberately destructive and inconvenient at that time was not without purpose or value.

In November 2016, Tennessee residents and much of the U. S. grieved and prayed as fire raged through the Smoky Mountains National Park. Known as the Gatlinburg Fires, the fires destroyed 17,000 acres, 24,000 cabins, businesses and additional structures, and resulted in 14 deaths. One description indicated "it was a screaming monster of flame and heat and terror."

The initial fire had actually begun in an isolated area known as Chimney Tops. But a windstorm would whip it out of control to become the engulfing disaster that devoured much of the mountain area as well as inflicting massive damage in the town of Gatlinburg and other areas of Sevier County.

Climbing Higher

Ironically in the days following the fire, the community and outside supporters rallied and rose tall to come alongside victims and businesses. The rally cry became "Gatlinburg Strong!" Folks stepped up to comfort and encourage, offer physical assistance, and contribute financially. Out of the ashes came a fresh spirit of generosity and caring.

Today, a variety of plants and animals are thriving in the post fire forests. Mountain laurel, jewelweed, and native plant species are emerging in the bald, burned areas. Bats, black bear, bobcats, coyotes, fox, turkey, deer, and varieties of birds are also thriving in the aftermath of the blackened woods.

Like physical fires, the "fires" of trials and difficulties can leave a trail of destruction, discouragement, and depression. Losses and disappointments can devour us if we focus on the charred ruins of dreams or dashed hopes. But, also like physical fires, new life can emerge from the ashes if we bring them to God. His promise is to give beauty from ashes and praise for heaviness (Isaiah 61:3). Renewal and regrowth can also make us stronger and our faith more resilient. Trials can become a testimony that brings encouragement and hope to others.

Photo Credit:
Richard Harris,
Cherokee Hiking Club,
Recipient of the 2021
Benton MacKaye Association
Distinguished Service Award

HIKING QUOTE: "Fire is part of the life cycle's rhythm. And just as fires in the woods are often key to the reforestation, so the fiery circumstances of life are key to our growth." (Dee Appel, A Heart Awake to Beauty)

14

I Once Was Lost

For the son of man came to seek and to save the lost
(Luke 19:10 NIV)

I have enjoyed hiking in the woods for my entire life but couldn't find much time for it during my working career. When I retired, I began to hike frequently and also enjoyed volunteer trail work in the National Forests. By the year 2000, I had hiked or worked on all of the trails in the Big Frog Wilderness, as well as many other trails in the Ocoee and Tellico Ranger Districts of the Cherokee National Forest. As I hiked and worked on trails, I noticed a sharp peak about three miles north of Boyd Gap known as Panther Knob. There were no trails to the top of Panther Knob, so the only way to get there was to do what hikers refer to as bushwhacking. I have always enjoyed going off trail to see some geographical features that interest me.

Early one winter morning, I decided to go to the top of Panther Knob. I parked at the trailhead for the Rock Creek Trail and began my bushwhack immediately on a long-abandoned roadbed. After a while, I began to notice that the old roadbed was taking me away from Panther Knob. I decided to turn off the road and follow the top of a ridgeline. The problem with the ridgelines in the area is a lot of green briar tangles, so I had to do a lot of high stepping to get through. After a while, this ridge intersected another, so I turned to follow it to the base of Panther Knob. From that point, it was a steep climb to the top of Panther Knob. I enjoyed lunch at the top, but the trees blocked most of the good views.

Climbing Higher

After lunch, I started to make my way back to the trailhead by following my morning route. I descended the steep side of Panther Knob and started down the ridgeline full of briars. I didn't realize it at the time, but I missed a right turn down the spur ridge that led to the old road. I ended up in a flat branch bottom that was full of rhododendron tangles. I found that I was really close to U.S. 64 but having a hard time making any headway through the rhododendron. By this time, my legs were giving out, and it was getting dark. I decided that the best way out was to backtrack until I could see the side of the ridge leading to Boyd Gap. I headed for the ridge and got to Boyd Gap at just about dark. I remember starting to sing "Amazing Grace" as I walked to my truck: "I once was lost, but now I'm found."

Almost every hiker has a "lost" story. And thankfully, most also have a found-the-trail-and-made-it-out story! It is the in between adventure that makes it worth telling. But the true measure of eternity for folks is the recognition of lostness and the need for the right direction. That is where Jesus enters the picture with His pronouncement, "I am the way and the truth and the life. No one comes to the Father except through me." (John 14:6) No question. He is our true trail guide. And He is our Amazing Grace.

Story Credit: Ken Jones. Ken has received the Benton McKaye Outstanding Service, American Trails State Trail Worker, and USDA Forest Service Trail Service Awards.

15

Miracles On the Trail

*And they did all eat and were filled:
and they took up of the fragments
that remained twelve baskets full
(Matthew 14:20 KJV)*

Someone said, "I don't really know how to pray. I just get my cup of coffee in the morning, sit down at the table, and talk to the Lord like He is my best friend," I thought, "That is about the purest form of prayer that I can imagine!"

As someone who has done a lot of hiking alone, I can relate. I'm not really alone. Jesus is my hiking partner. He travels with me at my own pace, and He never leaves me. I talk to Him a lot, both silently and out loud. He has rescued me from troubles many times. Sometimes even with miracles! I'll never forget my special miracles. Especially these three:

About 20 years ago, I left home one crisp October morning. I had parked at the end of Basin Creek Road. I rock hopped up Basin Creek to the big waterfall. It was one of those rare and tremendous autumn days. From the waterfall, I bushwhacked my way on up to the Hogback Spur Trail and hiked out to Bullet Creek Road. It was getting close to dark, and I had intended to bushwhack across country again to my truck, but I knew better than to try it in the dark without a flashlight.

I said, "Lord, if I had a flashlight this would be a good mile shorter, but as it is, I will have to stick to my road walk, and I am plenty tired already." I had barely spoken those words when I looked down, and there in the roadside ditch was an orange flashlight! I thought, "There is no way this thing is going to

Climbing Higher

work," but when I picked it up and pushed the button, it was as bright as a new one! Thank you, Lord, for a mile saved on my tired legs!

Twenty years later, that light is still in my old Chevy truck. I couldn't throw it away for anything. It was my miracle!

One winter day, Ken Jones and I were going up the Cherohala Skyway. Our conversation turned to a problem we had been having getting into the Forest Service repeaters on recent workdays. I said to Ken, "I'm going to go online and see if I can find a longer antenna than these little rubber ducks that our radios come with."

Ken and I rode on up to Mud Gap, and we walked the top of John's Knob following the state line back to Stratton Meadows. We were turning rocks over on the state line, looking for another one of the state line stones that Preston Author had mentioned in his 1914 publication on Western North Carolina as being "within one half mile of Absalom Stratton's grave." Preston didn't say which side, and after several trips, running both sides, we still haven't found it.

We returned to our truck at Mud Gap and pulled down under and just past, the Skyway bridge over North River Road. We were eating lunch, as we sat on the tailgate, when I looked down in the high grass beside us and spied something. I exclaimed, "You're never going to guess what I see!" Jumping down and pulling it out of the weeds, I held up my long antenna! Ken said, "There is no way that is going to fit your radio!" They make all kinds to fit different manufacturers. Pulling my radio out of my pack, I unscrewed my rubber duck, and it was just made for it. I'm still using it years later, and it works a whole lot better. Thank you, Lord!

Miracles On the Trail

I've saved the best miracle for last. It was a terribly hot summer morning, and the trail crew was assigned to log out the Long Branch Trail between the Skyway and North River. There had been a recent burn along it, and the ground was black. Add that to the fact that we were on a steep side slope in the broad sunlight, and it was truly an unusually hot day. We had consumed our water entirely shortly after lunch time, and it was still a long way to our pickup point on North River. By the time we made it low enough down the trail to hear Long Branch, people were getting in trouble with dehydration.

Thirst makes folks do strange things, and the crew began plunging through the vegetation toward the sound of the moving water. By the time I arrived, a few were lapping water out of Long Branch. The rest of us had heard enough horror stories about giardia, and we knew that hogs carry it. There are a lot of hogs on Long Branch. We abstained. Crossing the creek and heading on through dense woods, I said, "Lord, we need help".

Almost immediately, I spied something yellow over in the woods and went to check it out. It was a big yellow water cooler of the type sometimes seen on the front of a work truck. It was heavy and I was almost afraid of what might be in it, but I still pulled off the lid. It was stuffed full of unopened, and still sealed, store-bought bottled water! There was enough for everyone, and bottles left over. Thank you, Lord!

Maybe these things could be explained. The flashlight probably slid out of the back of a pickup headed up Starr Mountain. Someone lost an antenna. And hunters, back in the winter, had probably left the water cooler in the woods. Still, I know that my Lord works through ways of providence too, and I believe these are nothing less than miracles.

The Bible is absolutely filled with miracle stories. It should be no surprise to Christ's followers that God still sends occasional glimpses of His supernatural provision, power, and protection.

Climbing Higher

We follow Him because Jesus is the way to peace, forgiveness, eternal life, and heaven, but what a fun boost it is to experience these stories of His presence and to be able to share our stories.

Story Credit: Tazz Reid, creator and narrator of *Weekly Word Outdoor Adventures*. His trail awards include the 1000 Hour Award by USFS, Trail Warrior Award by Trail Blazer Magazine, and the Ken Jones Award for Volunteer of the Year at Tellico District, CNF.

16

Nature Speaks

*But ask the animals and they will teach you,
or the birds in the sky and they will tell you;
or speak to the earth and it will teach you
(Job 12:7-8 NIV)*

Hikers, walkers, wanderers – the tug of the outdoors is powerful. And most who have a lifelong love affair with it become eternal students of it. There is an endless thirst for knowledge of the heavens, the creeks, rivers, oceans, the ground, and living creatures. The changing of the seasons never grows old.

The excitement of new (and often unexpected) discoveries rekindles a childlike delight in the world that surrounds us. There is always something to enjoy from rainy days to mushroom colonies. Butterflies and birds beg to be seen, heard, sometimes chased, and certainly photographed.

So many plants and flowers have been linked to legends and symbols, often declaring history, faith, or even health connections. Plant life was used to provide remedies for physical ailments, particularly by Indians and early settlers. Even today, certain herbs and plants are used or studied for cures and treatments. Consider a few:

- The redbud that flowers in early spring, close to Easter, is also called the Judas tree. The name derives from the belief this was the tree species Judas used to hang himself after betraying Jesus. The blooms themselves also contain edible vitamin C.

Climbing Higher

- The dogwood tree represents additional Easter legends. This tree is reputed to have provided the wood for the cross of Jesus. The four delicate white petals form the shape of a cross and the grouping of tiny yellow strands in the center of the flower resemble a crown of thorns.

- There are daffodils, also known as the trumpets of spring or the messengers of hope. They are believed to have been brought from Europe by early settlers.

- Green, heart-shaped leaf clusters that flourish in spring and summer have two names. One is heartleaf after their appearance. They are also known as little brown jugs after the purple bud that opens when the stem blossoms. It has been discovered these plants contain digitalis (heart meds).

- There is also an interesting wildflower called hearts-a-bustin'. When in bloom, tiny red pods spill over from inside at the opening of the flower. Although it is also known as "strawberry bush," it is not edible for humans or animals.

- One plant has a fun name that makes it memorable as well as descriptive. Jack-in-the-pulpit is so called because this perennial wildflower, to some, resembles the figure of a preacher leaning over his pulpit. Native Americans have used parts of this flower for food (another name is Indian turnip) and it has also been prepared as an ointment for treatment of injuries.

Nature Speaks

Jesus often used nature to illustrate a story or drive home a lesson. The tiny mustard seed provided a commentary on God's generous response to even a small amount of faith (Matthew 17:20). He detailed the importance of our correct response to God's message through his sermon in Matthew 13 about the condition of the soil where truth (seeds) landed. Even the Old Testament references "oaks of righteousness" with a firm foundation (Isaiah 61) and compares a man who trusts God to a well-rooted tree (Jeremiah 17). No wonder we are told that creation declares God's presence. And who more than a hiker would be driven to worship the Creator?

Story Credit: *Weekly Word Outdoor Adventures*
(Tazz Reid/Susan Holmes)

Heartleaf

Jack N Pulpit

Climbing Higher

*Deep calls to deep
in the roar of your waterfalls
(Psalm 42:7 NIV)*

17

Sharing the Joy

*This is the day which the Lord hath made;
we will rejoice and be glad in it
(Psalms 118:24 KJV)*

As a recent widow from Mississippi, my 71-year-old grandmother came to visit our family in Maine for the summer. The year was 1972. Although I knew her as "Grandmother," her name was actually Alabama "Thelma" Walker Floyd. She had always seemed so old, and since I was only 19, I really considered her to be elderly. In many ways she was – her hair was always pulled up in a bun on her head, and her hair was its natural gray. Grandmother was not an active person and was more likely to be sitting reading her Bible, crocheting, or sewing. She was very soft-spoken although I feel that probably changed when she was in the pulpit. I'm sure she never wore a pair of pants in her entire life, so all activity was in a dress.

Grandmother enjoyed new experiences and wanted to see a moose in its natural habitat. We traveled to Baxter State Park to take a short hike to Sandy Brook Pond where moose could be spotted feeding in the early evening. An eight-mile ride at 20 mph on a narrow dirt road took us to the trailhead. The trail was packed earth with rocks and tree roots to maneuver. Some boggy areas had log crossings and others were just mucky spots. Grandmother found a broken pine stick to help steady herself.

As we approached the pond, multiple narrow paths with scratchy brush led to the water. Before seeing our first moose, Grandmother declared that she smelled a "cow." A moose had passed ahead of us. That short hike was not a disappointment as we saw multiple moose at the edge of the pond. They were feeding in the water, heads and racks dipping into the water and

Climbing Higher

coming up dripping with vegetation. Across the pond, Mount Katahdin and adjoining peaks rose up to the sky. This short excursion was a memorable experience for Grandmother and myself.

Sometimes the greater blessing of a trail is sharing it. Being able to experience with someone else the joy of discovery of a place we love increases in a fresh way our own appreciation and wonder as we see it anew through different eyes. That is also true with opportunities to share our faith and the story of what God has done in our lives.

The New Testament is full of the excitement associated with redeemed folks sharing their changed lives and salvation story with everyone around them. They couldn't be silent even when told to. No wonder when Jesus was told to rebuke those disciples that were praising Him, He responded by saying, "I tell you if they keep quiet, the stones will cry out." (Luke 19:40 NIV) Good news, like good trails, is meant to be shared.

Story and Photo Credit: James E. Floyd

HOOKED ON HIKING

A new acquaintance asked, "Why do you hike?" I responded to that question with all the intensity I reserved for talking about my favorite activity. "There is nothing like being outdoors. Besides, a person can hike the same trail, and it will always look different. They change with every season and even look different coming and going." But, I'm an avid advocate of hiking for a number of reasons.

- HIKING IS HEALTHY. Hiking offers great body benefits. It contributes to weight loss, strengthens bones, lowers blood pressure, and can also help control blood sugar. Even the sunlight from being outside helps the body activate its ability to manufacture vitamin D.

- HIKERS ARE HAPPIER. Physical activity can fight depression as well as lower stress levels. Exercise elevates a brain chemical called serotonin that actually acts as a mood booster. All of that makes hiking invigorating!

- HIKING IS CHEAP. There is very little expense involved in hiking. Good boots, a waist belt or backpack, a walking stick, and sometimes money for parking fees will cover most necessities. There is seldom an admission charge to incredible waterfalls, panoramic views, or the incomparable natural scenery.

- HIKING IS VERSATILE. Go alone or with friends. Choose a long trail or take a quick hike. Drive a while or find a trail close to home. Push yourself with a steep, strenuous trail or relax on a leisurely, easy path.

- HIKING SPANS THE SEASONS. Trails change with the calendar. They go from flowers and lush greens to crisp and multicolored to brown and bare, providing amazing visibility.

Climbing Higher

- HIKING IS SPIRITUAL. The outdoors is filled with the declaration of God's presence. Walking in that world, surrounded by the woods and the wildness, can feed our souls. It is in there; we can often think clearer or find peace ... or just feel sheer joy in the wonder of it all.

- HIKING BUILDS BONDS. My Mother's Day present from my sons is the gift of a hike. I choose the trail, and they join me. My husband and I hike regularly together, and I sometimes introduce friends to new trails. We often see families hiking and even grandparents bringing their grandchildren along. Sharing a walk along a mountain path can bring a fresh closeness to relationships.

- HIKING ADDS ADVENTURE. It's true that hiking can be an adventure. Spotting snakes or bears, getting lost, wading a creek, even taking a fall can be part of hiking a trail. Most incidents end happily and fuel conversations for days.

A famous hiker and trailblazer, John Muir, expressed so well the tug of a trail for a hiker. "Climb the mountains and get their good tidings. Nature's peace will flow into you as sunshine flows into trees. The winds will blow their own freshness into you, and the storms their energy, while cares will drop away from you like the leaves of Autumn." Who needs a better reason to hike?

*Trail Adventures*

Climbing Higher

Diary of a Hike
Liz and Logan

Liz: "Back in Seattle and really missing this view. One of the hardest hikes I've ever done, and one of the easiest decisions I've ever made. Can't wait to stop saying goodbye to this man."

Logan: "Went to the bottom of the Grand Canyon with a girlfriend. Came out the next day with a fiancé!"

June 18, 2016
An excellent wife who can find? She is far more precious than jewels (Proverbs 31:10 ESV)

It's surreal that I get to be married to this rock star momma and dad to these three little men. I'm an abundantly blessed man.

18

Here Hikes the Bride!

*Then the angel said to me, "Write this:
Blessed are those who are invited
to the wedding supper of the Lamb"
(Revelation 19:9 NIV)*

If trail shelters could talk, imagine the stories they would tell. They could share secrets about the hikers who stumble or sprint into their welcoming space. They would recount the hundreds of creatures that surround their territory and share stories of encounters between those creatures and weary hikers. They could even relate the colorful conversations that take place in earshot of their walls.

But the Windsor Furnace Shelter in Pennsylvania would have a special story to tell . . . of a romance and a wedding.

Robert Lahneman had attempted an Appalachian Trail thru-hike in 1993 but had to postpone plans after contracting Lyme disease. His later return to The Pinnacle in Pennsylvania was life-changing in a different way.

Robert met Robin Fletcher's brother and dad at The Pinnacle, and they gave him directions to the shelter where he rested for a while. Robin, also at the shelter, was impressed with Robert and hated to see him leave.

As fate would have it, Robert didn't leave. Apparently distracted, he ended up in the "wrong" parking lot. Which happened to be the right parking lot for Robin! Recognizing the Fletcher's license plate, Robert left a cordial note with his number and address.

Climbing Higher

The couple began dating and hiking together. Eight months later, he knelt on the floor of the Windsor Furnace Shelter and proposed. Where would one expect the wedding to take place? Of course, the shelter!

Oh, yes, if shelters could talk!

Brides in the Bible also show up in unusual places. The first one, Eve, got to help manage the Garden until trouble came to Paradise. Rebecca was brought to Isaac by a servant leading her camel. Ruth came to Boaz when her mother-in-law played Cupid on the threshing floor of his business.

Jesus is also waiting on His bride. Those who have loved and followed Him have invitations to a marriage supper. Heaven is the ultimate destination wedding! Are you invited?

19

A "Lucky" Miracle?

But He knows the way that I take
(Job 23:10 NIV)

Carolyn Dorn, 52, from South Carolina, set out alone in early December for a two-week camping trip to the Gila Wilderness in Albuquerque, New Mexico. But when she ended up on the wrong side of the Gila River, things went terribly wrong. Rain and snow created a surging river, and she became trapped.

Carolyn's car was spotted two and a half weeks after she left. After an intense search failed to locate her, the attempt to find her ended. But two weeks after that, Albert and Peter Kottke, brothers and university students, heard a slight sound as they hiked out of the wilderness. They saw a woman across the river, moving slowly. It had been five weeks since Ms. Dorn entered the wilderness.

The brothers gave food, firewood, water, and reading material to the weak hiker (she would need to wait at least two more nights for rescue). Then, they hiked 20 miles out for help.

After receiving the marked location, a New Mexico National Guard helicopter swooped in for the rescue. Frankie Benoist, the search and rescue coordinator, called Carolyn Dorn's survival a miracle. Albert Kottke stated, "It was luck we took a longer route and went by her campsite, and it was luck that she saw us and called out."

The Bible might offer further explanation for the rescue of Carolyn Dorn. It would tell us that God orders our steps (Proverbs 20:24), and we can trust that He ordered the steps of the Kottke brothers exactly where they needed to be for the rescue He had planned. He also sustains us, so He was the One who gave Carolyn strength and endurance as she waited for rescue. He is the One who is "mighty to save" (Zephaniah 3:17), and He did. "Luck?" Not likely. "Miracle?" Most probably. Why did He allow her five-week wilderness saga? Why couldn't the first rescuers locate her? Perhaps we can find Paul's answer in Romans 11: "O the depth of the riches both of the wisdom and knowledge of God! How unsearchable are his judgements and his ways past finding out!" (KJV)

WISE WORDS:
"There are only two ways to live your life.
One is as though nothing is a miracle.
The other is as though everything is a miracle."
(Albert Einstein)

20

Chasing a Dream

They said to one another,
"Here comes this dreamer!"
(Genesis 3:19 NASB)

In winter 2008, James Anderson caught the dream he had been chasing. He, along with some friends, climbed Mount Kilimanjaro, the tallest mountain on the continent of Africa.

Although this mountain has an altitude of 19,000 feet and the trails are at 45-degree angles, ropes are not necessary to reach the summit, and Mr. Anderson wanted to climb rope free. Planning for the climb took a year. Then the group of four flew to a tiny village called Moshi where they met their guide, Emanuel. They were required by law to have a guide.

They completed preparations in a culture of poverty and mud huts where meal preparation took place over open fires. James Anderson observed, "It was incredible how the villagers of Moshi lived. Yet they seemed happy, always smiling."

The seven-day climb took place in 10 to 15-degree temperatures, with the wind chill dropping it even lower. Even with three pairs of gloves, their hands were painfully cold, and one climbing buddy experienced ongoing numbness in his fingers. Anderson acknowledged, "You get to a point where you want to quit, so it's an act of the will to keep going." But he remembers reaching the top as the sun rose over the horizon. Mission accomplished . . . dream realized.

Any regrets? "I'm really glad I did it. It has enriched my life."

In his book, **The 21 Indispensable Qualities of a Leader**, *John C. Maxwell asked, "What do you dream of? In your wildest*

Climbing Higher

imagination, what do you see yourself doing? Now, what is standing between you and your dream?"

Dreams are the stuff life is made of. Truly pursuing dreams is not so common. But we have been created with longings and gifts that often line up with our dreams. Our highest longing for relationship is met in a commitment to Jesus Christ. Our longing for purpose and significance is found in contribution to a legacy beyond ourselves. Even the pursuit of our passions can confirm how God has shaped us.

So, dust off those dreams. Start chasing them. If discouragement sets in, echo the confidence of the Psalmist: "All my longings lie open before you, Lord; my sighing is not hidden from you." (Psalm 38:9 NIV) And keep following hard after those dreams.

Story Credit: James Anderson, Cherokee Hiking Club

HIKING QUOTE:
"Go confidently in the direction of your dreams. Live the life you have imagined."
(Henry David Thoreau)

21

Two Joshuas

*For the Lord thy God,
He it is that doth go with thee
(Deuteronomy 36:6 KJV)*

Perhaps one of the youngest hikers to ever take off through the woods on his own was three-year-old Joshua Childers. In May 2009, Joshua walked away from his home near Arcadia, Missouri, on a Monday near lunch time. His dad was asleep, and his mom was on the phone. Later, he told his grandmother that he was on his way to visit her. She lived about five miles away.

The small home Joshua walked away from happened to border the wild terrain of the Mark Twain National Forest. The area provided habitat for bears, mountain lions and snakes. And at the time of Joshua's "hike," heavy rains were raising the creek levels.

By the second day of the search for Joshua, rescuers were pessimistic. Their survival hopes were dim for the little boy wondering through that environment with no food or water, dressed only in pull-ups and sneakers. Still, hundreds of volunteers were on the scene, as well as professional rescue crews, planes, divers, and sonar. Dogs, horses, all-terrain vehicles, and even donkeys scattered throughout the area surrounding Joshua's home.

Then, it happened! A volunteer searcher spotted a child's bare bottom lying on the ground near a creek. The volunteer called out, not certain if Joshua was alive. But covered with ticks and wearing only one shoe, Joshua sat up, smiled, and assured his

Climbing Higher

rescuer he was ready to leave the woods. He was only half a mile from his grandmother's home.

The Bible tells the story of another Joshua. He was like little Joshua in some ways. Leading multitudes of Israelites, he knew where he was going. It wasn't Grandma's, but the Promised Land . . . the new home God was giving His people. Also, perhaps like three-year-old Joshua, he was a little anxious. God told him to "be strong and courageous because I am with you." Adam Childers, Joshua's relieved dad, said, "You doubt if God's actually with you for a while, and then something like this happens and you know He's there."

For those needing company on their trail, that is good to know.

22

Bug Eaters

*And the same John had his raiment of camel's hair . . .
and his meat was locusts and wild honey.
(Matthew 3:4 KJV)*

Unlike some gourmets who do include an occasional grasshopper or ant in their diet, Derek Mamoyac never expected he would survive on insects in his October 2008 hike up Mount Adams in southern Washington. Mamoyac had begun the hike up the 11,657-foot Pikers Peak before dawn, only to decide that the fierce wind and the ice chips in his eyes demanded a surrender to the elements and a turn around on the trail.

However, on his way down, he slipped, resulting in a fall and a broken ankle. When he did not show up for work, family members reported him missing and the search began. Meanwhile, Derek crawled through the snow looking for a trail that he knew circled the mountain. He believed making it to the trail would enable searchers to find him.

In his five nights alone, crawling on the mountain, Derek ate centipedes that tasted like Doritos, and ants reminiscent of spicy, hot tamales. He also consumed berries and mushrooms while drinking from nearby creeks.

When the hiker was finally rescued, he said he didn't let himself consider that he wouldn't be rescued. Derek understood that "Surviving, beating the odds, requires believing in the impossible."

There was a New Testament character described in Matthew 3:4 as regularly eating insects. We are told that the diet of John the Baptist was locusts and wild honey. John was a rough kind of

Climbing Higher

character who lived in the Judean wilderness. No doubt, hiking was a lifestyle. But, unlike Derek, he wasn't lost, waiting to be found. On the contrary, he was looking himself – for the One who would follow after him. And he did believe in what many thought was impossible.

He believed the One who was coming would redeem not only John's people, the Jewish nation, but would also bring salvation to the world. John was right, too. He not only got to welcome the Christ (Jesus) and baptize him, but the locust eater from the wilderness also received high praise from Jesus as the "greatest man born to a woman." Wow!

23

Sleeping With a Bear

*I will lie down and sleep in peace,
for you alone, O Lord,
make me dwell in safety
(Psalms 4:8)*

Most long-time hikers have an animal story or two. Burl Maupin is no exception. His story took place in 1974 at McGhee Spring – a backcountry campsite in North Carolina. Anxious to try out a new external frame backpack, he made the four-mile hike in with a friend who didn't plan to stay the night.

After his friend left, Burl set up his plastic tube tent and cooked hamburgers in his Boy Scout mess kit. He poured the grease on a nearby stump.

As dusk settled, Burl spotted a form in the distance. In his words, "It was a big bear stretching its nose straight up as high as it could. It smelled me and my grease. There was no getting away."

Burl made the choice to settle in but also to prepare for the bear. He moved quietly, finding a weapon, building up the fire, and putting his food out of reach. Meanwhile, the bear moved close enough for Burl to hear it breathing and smell its pungent fur. He now acknowledged, "This was real. That was a bear. Was it going to eat me? It was me and the bear in the great outdoors."

Burl's story continues as the bear joined him for the night. His "guest" ate his food and took his backpack. It also nibbled Burl's toes and sniffed his head. The campsite was ransacked until "nothing was left, but me," Burl comments. At dawn, Burl

Climbing Higher

eased out of the campsite and walked barefoot to a stream. As he returned, he heard his visitor grunt and watched as three cubs descended a nearby tree. All four bears walked away.

Burl's decision to remain calm and even passive may have saved his life. Because he did not panic, he had a once-in-a-lifetime experience.

Life often brings tough, unexpected circumstances, and we have choices to make. We can panic, flee, fall apart, and just abandon ship. Or we can trust God to bring good out of even the toughest times. He specializes in making "all things work together for good" and teaching us how to give thanks in everything by revealing Himself in unpredictable places.

Burl reflects, "I would gladly give a little sleep, some comfort, some equipment, and some food to do it again."

> BURL REFLECTS:
> "I would gladly give a little sleep, some comfort, some equipment, and some food to do it again."

24

Pick Your Guide

The Lord will guide you always (Isaiah 58:11 NIV)

Daniel Mazur almost made it. He was only two hours away from the summit of Mount Everest when his climb was disrupted, and his goal thwarted.

Mazur, an American guide, was climbing the world's highest peak with another guide and two paying clients on May 26, 2006, when they came across Lincoln Hall, a British climber. Mr. Hall had been "left" there the day before because his guides had thought he was dead!

When Mazur's group found Hall, he was sitting up. But he had no equipment, no oxygen, no gloves, hat or sleeping bag. As the men approached, Mr. Hall commented, "I imagine you are surprised to see me here." Mazur's team made the decision to forfeit their own climb to the top and spent the next four hours preparing Hall for his rescue. They moved him back from the slopes and provided nourishment.

Although Mazur had scaled Mount Everest previously from the southern side, he did not complete this hike from the northern side. But that wasn't his greatest regret. "It was very disappointing for me to miss my chance at the summit, but even more that I could not get my job done." He had failed to take his clients to the top.

Lincoln Hall was abandoned by his guides and left for dead. Their mistake could have resulted in his death. But, mercifully, still another guide saved his life. By doing so, he also cost those he was guiding their trip to the top. While we would certainly applaud Mazur's decision, this story has two guides – neither of whom accomplished their mission.

Climbing Higher

But we have a guide who will never abandon us, will not make mistakes, and will certainly take us where we need to go. His presence as a cloud by day and fire by night guided Israel 40 years in their journey to Canaan. He took David from a shepherd's job to the king's palace. He led Job through incredible suffering to total restoration. We are told that He guides His people with His counsel, with His right hand, and with His spirit. We can trust that God "will be our guide, even to the end." (Psalm 48:14)

Photo Credit: Snappy Johnson, Cherokee Hiking Club

HIKING QUOTE: "When a person says yes to the Lord and agrees to follow Him, God will move heaven and earth to help that person stay on His path. What God did for me on the Appalachian Trail was just a picture of what He longs to do for everyone who will walk with Him one step at a time." (Bill Erwin, *Blind Courage*, 1993)

HIKING TRIVIA: "Our guide made $15 a day and that was considered wealthy." (James Anderson, referring to the guide for his 2008 trip up Mt. Kilimanjaro)

25

Heroes

Let us fix our eyes on Jesus
(Hebrews 12:2)

His trail name was Tennessee Red. He was heading north on the Appalachian Trail after staying at the Maupin Fields Shelter in Virginia. It was the last shelter before reaching Shenandoah National Park. The day had been good.

While sitting on some rocks in the Tye River, he had noticed a big fish. Reaching his hand into the water, he actually caught it! He roasted the thirteen-inch prize over the shelter campfire, sharing it with another hiker.

Fresh from the fish fry and feeling pretty smug about his "catch," Tennessee Red proceeded on along the trail at Shenandoah. He soon came across a troop of Boy Scouts. They were fascinated with him and because they had a good food supply, he encouraged their friendship. But he needed to keep moving.

However, his hasty flight up the trail was interrupted by the presence of a BIG rattlesnake. With the Boy Scouts close behind, Tennessee Red decided to kill it and go.

No way. Tennessee Red, alias Snake Killer, was now an instant hero. He recalls, "they thought I was Daniel Boone reincarnated!" The Boy Scouts were charmed and needed to celebrate. They cut the snake open (revealing a deceased rat), skinned it, sliced it into three sections, and roasted it on sticks. Pictures were taken, and later, others on the trail recognized Tennessee Red from those pictures.

Climbing Higher

He still has the rattlesnake skin attached to his hiking stick. It's a memento of his "moments of fame."

Heroes appear in the most unexpected places. A passerby rescues someone from a burning building, a child calls 911 and saves a parent. Normal people perform acts of courage or sacrifice, a scientist discovers a cure, a soldier saves his comrades . . . and an unlikely person bears the label of hero.

The Bible has its own Hall of Fame, its own list of unlikely heroes. They appear in Hebrews 11 and include a shipbuilder called Noah, a shepherd and murderer named Moses, Daniel, who was a prisoner of war, and Rahab, a prostitute from Jericho.

These heroes had some common threads. God was not ashamed to be called their God. They had gained approval through their faith, and He has prepared a city for them.

Still, Christ followers have one hero, one they aspire to emulate. He is the One who made Himself, not a hero, but "nothing" (Philippians 2:7). He is the One who stepped down from heaven to connect us to God.

Photo Credit: James Anderson, Cherokee Hiking Club

26

Wild No More

*The wolf will live with the lamb,
the leopard will lie down with the goat,
the calf and the lion and the yearling together;
and a little child will lead them. (Isaiah 11:6 NIV)*

In spring 2006, Tennesseans were stunned by a black bear attack that led to the death of a six-year-old girl. The bear initially attacked her two-year-old brother. When the mother came to the aid of her son, the bear targeted her. The terrified six-year-old ran away. In the chaos of helping the two who were injured, time passed before it was discovered that the bear had captured and killed the little girl. The attack occurred near a popular, much-frequented waterfalls trail and camping area. Bears had never been a serious concern for families enjoying the recreation facility.

There is no satisfactory explanation for the circumstances of the attack or knowledge of what might have triggered the tragedy. Although two bears were captured and evaluated to determine if one of them had killed the victim, nothing conclusive was discovered. Much of the event remains a tragic mystery.

That same spring, there were three alligator attacks in Florida, resulting in two deaths. And in Illinois, a deer turned violent and attacked three people!

Persons who choose not to hike often express alarm and fear about the possibility of animal attacks or snake bites. They can't imagine anyone would choose to expose themselves to that danger. While such events are very rare, they do occur

Climbing Higher

occasionally. But then again, bears sometimes wander into neighborhoods, and snakes slither around our yards.

It is so true that life on this earth can be a scary place. But believers have hope of a different kind of future. Isaiah 11 gives promise of a day when animals that have been enemies will roam, rest, and even eat together, side by side. Small children can play near a cobra pit or a snake's den without fear of harm. And all will delight in the presence of the God who created it all.

Imagine being greeted on a mountain trail by a tail-wagging, wild boar or bending down to pet a friendly skunk! We are told in scripture that all creation groans as it waits for God to restore the earth to its former glory (Romans 8:19-22).

Even as we delight now in the amazing beauty and life abundant in nature, we can know so much more lies ahead for those who follow Christ. They will experience eternal life and dwell in God's new heaven and earth.

HIKING QUOTE: "The creation knows things are going to get better. Our world knows a moment of renewal is just around the corner. Carnivorous lions will eat lettuce and will curl up for naps with lambs and children. The stars will sing again, and all will be well in God's peaceable kingdom."
(Scott Hoezee, *Remember Creation*)

27

No Hiker Left Behind

I will even make a way in the wilderness
(Isaiah 43:19 KJV)

Phil's wife was excited to push his wheelchair along a trail at Tallulah Gorge State Park. The trail, made from recycled tires, allowed the couple to enjoy an amazing view of the canyon itself and some of the waterfalls.

Shela's dad carried her transport stroller up and down the steep rocky path at Fall Creek Falls in Pikeville, Tennessee. Even though she was wheelchair dependent and had no mobility, he was determined to allow his young daughter an up-close view of the 256-foot waterfall.

In 2011, 22-year-old Chelsea Fernandes was able to enjoy an independent hike as she navigated her own wheelchair through two and a half miles of mountain wilderness. At that time, Crocheted Mountain Rehabilitation Center in southern New Hampshire opened trails designed to provide easy access for people of all abilities. It is the longest accessible trail in a mountain environment.

The trails enabled hikers to cross boardwalks over wetlands, experience elevation climbs, cross through woods and meadows, and see blueberry fields, wildflowers and even wildlife. Paths are mostly made of recycled materials, including plastic bags. Chelsea was delighted to be able to "experience nature like everyone else."

The Forestry Service also provides accessible trails in Montana, New Mexico, West Virginia, and Michigan. The vision is catching on and accessibility is increasing, which creates a wonderful adventure for those with any type of challenge, and for their caregivers as well.

It is exciting to see new opportunities surface for those with challenges and for those who manage care for folks with challenges. It is especially delightful to observe them experiencing the joy of the outdoors and the many benefits that come with time outside.

God also delights to surprise His people with unanticipated paths and sometimes throws open wide, new doors in our daily lives:

- *Who would have imagined that Israel would have escaped the Egyptian army by walking a dry "trail" through the Red Sea while the waters paused around them? (Exodus 14:21-22)*
- *Or that a military leader with leprosy would be healed by the instructions of a stranger telling him to wash in muddy water? (2 Kings 5)*
- *Or believe that a little boy would kill his country's most powerful enemy with a "sling and a stone"? (1 Samuel 17)*
- *That a young Jewish girl would become a queen just in time to save her people from mass murder? (Esther 4:14)*

There is a song that says, "God will make a way where there seems to be no way." We are told that nothing is impossible with God. Perhaps we can find comfort and hope in remembering the challenge of Proverbs 3:5-6 that if we choose to acknowledge Him in all our ways, He will direct our paths.

28

Trails, Toilets, and Happy Endings

Before they call I will answer; while they are still speaking I will hear (Isaiah 65:24 NIV).

The outing began like it would any other time a group of eight women decide to tackle the famous Le Conte trail system in the Smoky Mountains for a stay at the legendary lodge. It is a rustic and basic inn with breathtaking views for those blessed to be able to reserve overnight rooms and meals after their 6400-foot climb to the peak.

Andrea Coulter and her hiking companions were finally able to experience the April hike as part of her, courtesy of COVID, delayed and postponed birthday celebration. Getting to the top was a typical climb of girl talk, fun, and the challenge of the trail. There was nothing unexpected about the weather, just a usual Tennessee mountain spring day containing sunshine, rain, sleet, and a little snow.

What was a little more memorable was the trek out the following day. It was one of those serendipity times when God showed up to remind them His eye is on the sparrow . . . and on a group of His daughters experiencing "peculiar" calamities.

It was near the trail exit that the usual potty spot became one source of alarm. Because when the car keys needed for the return trip home actually landed in the pit toilet itself, it presented a dilemma. Andrea's unusual observation? "The toilet had been well used so the fact that the toilet paper was piled high proved to be a plus." Still, even the resourceful use of their hiking sticks did not retrieve the keys.

At the point of desperation and brain drain, God apparently came to the rescue - in the incredibly timely appearance of a trash truck! The shovel on the truck quickly provided the

Climbing Higher

necessary implement for acquiring the evasive keys. And Andrea's possession of a large container of hand sanitizer certainly proved to be a plus.

But the day's excitement was not over. As the relieved crew made their way home through Townsend, Tennessee, one of the passengers received a phone call with a question for another passenger (related parties). "Do you know where your cell phone and wallet are?" She didn't!

As "circumstances" would have it, one of the group had dropped her jacket, containing her cell phone and wallet, on the trail. What were the chances that the family picking it up would know them and be able to contact the husband whose phone call alerted his wife to the location of her lost . . . now found . . . jacket, phone, and wallet?

Truly, absolutely, on this adventure God had worked overtime on and off the trail for His hiking ladies.

God sometimes does choose to intervene in dramatic ways in even the small affairs of our days. The Psalmist says He will accomplish what concerns us (Psalms 138). We are also told that He goes before us, and behind us, and hems us in (Psalms 139). It is wonderful training to recognize His presence, give thanks, and share our stories with each other.

Story and Photo Credit: Andrea Richardson Coulter

Trail Lessons

Climbing Higher

HIKING HINTS

1. Put together a small first-aid kit with emergency supplies.
2. Dress wisely for the weather and keep lightweight rain gear in your backpack.
3. Always leave information regarding your location with someone.
4. Keep a trail map and compass, especially for new trails.
5. Shoes are important, get a good fit.
6. Go easy on the land, leave no trace of trash or careless plundering.
7. Remember to carry water and easy energy food like trail mix, fruit, or nuts.

29

Breaking The Rules

*So the law was put in charge
to lead us to Christ that
we might be justified by faith.
(Galatians 3:24 NIV)*

They were five strangers, about to become friends and partners in adventure. The group was part of a conference near Black Mountain, North Carolina, when they impulsively decided to take an early evening hike on a trail leading to Rattlesnake Summit. Because of a black bear warning, it was best to travel in groups. That was probably the only thing they did right.

The primary hiking rule is to always let someone know where you are going. Common sense rules would call for a flashlight in approaching darkness and at least a small water supply. Appropriate shoes are also helpful. These hikers did none of the above.

Mercifully, the uphill hike to the summit wasn't terribly long and only moderately difficult. It was accomplished without incident and the view was glorious, well worth the effort. But darkness was setting in. On the descent, the group somehow separated into sets of two and three.

While chattering away, one group passed the turn-off leading to the trail's end. The other group made the correct turn, then stopped to wait for their stragglers. Eventually, the two groups communicated by cell phone, but both got "lost" coming out in the darkness.

Climbing Higher

Thankfully, the area was civilized with some lighting and the delays were only an inconvenience. But to at least one hiker, it was a reminder that breaking the rules is never a good idea.

God gave man a set of rules to follow. They are called the Ten Commandments. But the true purpose of those rules was to prove to us that we are, by nature, rule-breakers, not capable of perfectly adhering to God's standards.

Paul indicates in Galatians 3 that the Ten Commandments are a schoolmaster that lead us to Christ. When we see our own inability to do right, it condemns us. We know then we need another way to be right with God. Then we turn to Jesus, "the way, and the truth, and the life." Coming to relationship with Him frees us from the condemnation of the rules we cannot keep. He puts His presence within us and gives us power to follow Him.

When the hiking group broke the rules, the results could have been tragic. When we break God's rules and fail to acknowledge we need Jesus, the results **will** *be tragic --- we will be separated from Him forever.*

HIKING QUOTE: "The influence of fine scenery, the presence of mountains, appeases our irritations and elevates our friendships." (Ralph Waldo Emerson, Culture, The Conduct of Life, 1860)

30

Decisions, Decisions!

*If any of you lacks wisdom, he should ask God,
who gives generously to all without finding fault,
and it will be given to him. (James 1:5)*

They had been married 65 years. Now, in their mid-eighties, their greatest adventure was still ahead. Corky and Evelyn Scott left their campsite at Elkmont Campground in the Smoky Mountains for a "brief" hike. They had already hiked short sections of the trail which they felt certain looped quickly back to the campground. Confident the hike wouldn't last long, they didn't take food or water.

A beautiful day made the leisurely hiking relaxing and enjoyable. But when a trail marker indicated they were a good distance from the camp, Evelyn began to express doubt that their trail looped back after all. Corky, however, felt compelled to finish the trail and persuaded his weary wife to keep going.

Several hours later, another sign now indicated they were 10 miles from their camp! As darkness closed in, so did storm clouds. They sought shelter under a tree as thunder and lightning turned their pleasant hike into a fearful foray. They huddled together through the night as the rain raged around them.

With the arrival of morning, decisions had to be made. They had been without food and water for 24 hours. Evelyn could now walk only a few steps at a time.

Giving his wife strict instructions to stay near the trail, Corky reluctantly set off alone to find help. They each spent a second night on the trail before Corky made his way out in early morning to alert the rangers. Skeptical that the couple could

Climbing Higher

have possibly gone as far as Corky indicated, they were amazed to find Evelyn exactly where he said she should be.

They discovered Evelyn had slept 24 hours after Corky left, waking just in time to face her rescuers.

Our lives are filled with decisions, both big and small. We choose how to dress, who to marry, where to live, what to do with our lives. One decision can sometimes alter our lives forever. Corky and Evelyn's adventure contained wise and foolish decisions. To hike an uncertain trail without food or water wasn't wise. But Corky's choice to go for help and Evelyn's wisdom in staying put led to a happy ending. Our endings may not always be happy, but those who follow Christ have a Wonderful Counselor who tells us to ask for wisdom.

> QUOTING CORKY: "I learned a lot of things on that hike. The most important is that when Evelyn says we ought to turn around, we really ought to turn around."

31

Learning The Hard Way

A wise man thinks ahead.
(Proverbs 13:16 TLB)

It was August of 1966. Ann Hysinger Gray describes herself as a "naïve 22" when she headed out from Nashville with two friends to conquer a mountain trail in the Smokies. In her own words, Ann acknowledges, "None of us had done the hike before. No one was prepared – no hiking boots or sticks and no flashlights. I don't think any of us had any concept of a five-mile hike UP a mountain."

Ann's group hung out in Gatlinburg shopping part of the day before hitting the trail . . . in their tennis shoes instead of hiking boots. After walking what seemed to be *nearly* two miles, they passed a sign indicating they had completed only one-half mile. Reality set in and so did darkness as the trio continued their evening "jaunt" to the lodge at the top of the mountain.

Eventually, the lodge sent employees to locate their missing hikers and lead them in. They didn't arrive in time for their hearty evening meal and had to be content with warm soup. They also had no proof of their adventure or their beautiful surroundings – no one bothered to take a camera (in the days before cell phones).

Now, older and wiser, Ann still has vivid memories of her experience. She indicates, "I have since climbed that trail three more times and was much better prepared (hiking boots and a stick, along with a backpack, water, and snacks). I have really enjoyed those climbs.

Climbing Higher

Luckily, other than some minor physical discomforts and feeling pretty foolish, Ann and her friends suffered no ongoing trauma related to their lack of preparation for hiking the mountain. That isn't always the case. Stories are often told of unprepared hikers getting lost or falling victim to weather conditions.

We are also warned in the Scriptures about the consequences of being unprepared. Lack of preparation may result in lost opportunities, tragic regrets, or could even cost eternal fellowship with God. In the book of Daniel, King Nebuchadnezzar failed to heed God's warning and turn to Him. He wasn't "ready." He lost his sanity and his kingdom until he acknowledged God. But in Genesis 41, the Pharoah of Egypt allowed Joseph to prepare Egypt for an approaching famine and saved many lives.

All of us need to prepare for eternity by trusting in Jesus who is "the way, the truth, and the life." Then, we need to prepare to follow His call and purposes for our lives, whatever that entails. Are you prepared?

HIKING QUOTE:
"The Trail will ALWAYS be a Pain-in-the-Neck.
The Trail will ALWAYS be
　　too steep and descend too far.
In fact, The Trail will NEVER make you happy,
　　unless you are happy just being on the trail."
　　　　(Swan, AT thru-hiker)

32

Traveling Light

*Life does not consist in
an abundance of possessions
(Luke 12:15 NIV)*

From 2001-2014, Winton Porter was the owner of The Crossings. He offered a hostel and outfitters services at Neel Gap near Blood Mountain for hikers on the Georgia section of the Appalachian Trail. One of the services he provided was assistance to hikers who needed to lighten their load of equipment and supplies. He then packaged and mailed home, items they needed to discard.

In his delightful book, *Just Passing Thru*, Porter references Ray Jardine, a brilliant aerospace engineer turned full-time adventurer. Jardine and his wife have hiked the "Triple Crown" of North America long distance trails: the Appalachian Trail, the Pacific Crest Trail, and the Continental Divide Trail.

Ray Jardine's passionate commitment to traveling light as a long-distance hiker resulted in his inventions of a variety of tools and principles for doing so. His book, *Beyond Backpacking*, is considered to have launched the ultralight backpacking movement.

Porter, however, isn't sure attempting ultralight backpacking is always a wise or safe decision for novice hikers. He often cautions them to that affect, but usually finds his counsel rejected. He is concerned that beginners who travel too light may compromise safety.

There is, however, one invitation to "travel light" that offers only relief and peace. Jesus also observed the tendency of people to carry more than they should or could. He was

Climbing Higher

referring to the rules and rituals that Israel's hypocritical religious leaders burdened the Jewish people with.

So, Jesus, who spent his life headed to crucifixion on the cross that would set them free, offered another alternative. It's the same one He extends to us. It is His solution for lightening our load. His invitation is "Come to me all you who are weary and burdened, and I will give you rest. Take my yoke upon you and learn from me . . . and you will find rest for your souls. For my yoke is easy and my burden is light." (Matthew 11:28-30 NIV)

To RSVP an acceptance to this invite is to share an adventure even long-distance hiking can't duplicate!

WISE WORDS: "The burlap bag of worry. Cumbersome. Chunky. Unattractive. Scratchy. Hard to get a handle on, irritating to carry, and impossible to give away."
    (Max Lucado, *Traveling Light*)

33

Trail Tragedies

*The light shines in the darkness and
the darkness has not overcome it.
(John 1:5 NIV)*

It is not unexpected for longtime hikers to experience falls, illness, injuries, or insect bites. They will even come across an occasional snake. What they don't anticipate in their escape from civilization is to become victims of crime. And it rarely happens. But some hikers have indeed had their adventures forever marred by unforgettable encounters with man at his worst.

In the summer of 2008, a young Blood Mountain hiker was kidnapped and lost her life at the hands of a serial killer later discovered to be responsible for other trail murders. The hiking community, and America in general, was shocked at the terror that had occurred on this well-traveled trail.

In 1978, four teenagers on a summer backpacking trip along the Appalachian Trail from Roan Mountain to Damascus, Virginia, were subjected to brutal assaults from five drunken assailants. Their tragedy actually resulted in escalation of a delayed change to that portion of the trail. But the crimes robbed the victims of their joy of hiking for years.

Several, in later years, returned to the place of their attack to recover what had been lost on that fateful hike. One, who had experienced the bondage of that past fear, placed a cross on a nearby tree. It was her symbol that she had "reclaimed that mountain," understanding that finally, "love had worked to undo the effects of evil."

Climbing Higher

This hiker turned victim, turned overcomer had discovered the secret to healing from the tragedy: receiving the redeeming and restoring work that took place on the cross. She allowed the One who "so loved the world" to replace the aftermath of evil with the power of faith.

Evil surrounds us. Most of us will experience it, though perhaps to a lesser degree than these victims. But there is One who tells us, "I have overcome the world" (John 16:33) and instructs us to "overcome evil with good." (Romans 12:21)

HIKING QUOTE: "Everybody needs beauty as well as bread, places to play in and pray in, where nature may heal and give strength to body and soul." (John Muir)

WISE WORDS: "Much of what has been rattled apart within our souls by this brutal world somehow gets quietly reassembled in the face of God's handiwork." (Scott Hoezee, Remember Creation)

34

Along The Way

You are no longer strangers and foreigners
(Ephesians 2:19 NKJV)

When Regina Jay and her sister, Tammy Neely, began their 500-mile trek across Spain on the Camino de Santiago, they each had hopes of resolution from personal pain. However, Regina recounts a different discovery on this path that is often referred to as "The Way."

She mentions following the ancient trail through small villages, over mountains and hills, and across the plains of Spain. She indicates, "I was enthralled by the majesty of cathedrals and entranced by templars, old Roman bridges and flower filled villages. But in the midst of that beauty and the physical challenge of the walk itself, I experienced something even more wondrous."

It was the people . . . varied nationalities, all seeking holy moments, divine inspiration, or clarity of some kind. It was a work challenging the soul as well as the body. They came from Boston, Ireland, Australia, Norway, even Tennessee! There were those disappointed in their experiences with God, others that were agnostic, atheist, or some just seeking to know God better. The encounters offered opportunity for dialogue, encouragement, and friendship. "After all," Regina commented, "the habit of people sharing a journey is to talk about why they are on it."

Regina's own spiritual breakthrough came at Cruz de Ferro (the Iron Cross), a traditional place for the laying down of burdens. She placed a memorial rock to declare her own release. But she completed the memorable pilgrimage with a fresh appreciation

Climbing Higher

for the lives and stories surrounding her and the ongoing opportunities for connecting along "the way."

People take to trails for a huge variety of reasons. For some, it is a passion for the outdoors and all that includes. For others, it is a quest for the physical reward of pushing the body forward. Still, more find that hiking rewards the soul as well as the body. The trail that Regina completed is one that is often considered a spiritual journey. While on it, she discovered the truth of a wonderful quote that says, "Our lives are story shaped, and we knead them into bread to feed each other."

Jesus intended us to live aware of the stories and needs of those around us. After His death, resurrection, and ascension to heaven, He established the church to be a community that would share His love, presence, and hope with each other and the world. For all its flaws, the church is still a place filled with stories of forgiveness, restoration, and redemption.

*After all, He **is** "THE WAY, the truth, and the life." (John 14:6).*

WISE WORDS:
"Life is a steep climb, and it does the heart good to have somebody 'call back' and cheerily beckon us on up the high hill. We are all climbers together, and we must help one another."
(Mrs. Charles E. Cowman, Streams in the Desert)

35

A Helping Hand

*Two are better than one . . .
if one falls down, his friend can help him up
(Ecclesiastes 4:9-10 NIV)*

Dr. Beverly Rose, a writer who is trapped in her body by a rare neuromuscular disease, shared a story of her first wheelchair hike. The big balloon tires on her custom-designed wheelchair allowed her to move up the mountain, accompanied by a friend.

The season was fall and she was anticipating with much excitement the view that awaited her at the summit. But right before the peak, a sharp ascent in the trail halted the wheelchair ride. Still, Dr. Rose could not give up her pursuit. Requesting the assistance of her doubtful friend, she insisted she would "climb" the rest of the way. Leaning on her friend, they hiked together to the top.

Her memory of that event carried her through some truly rough days. After describing the glorious view at the summit, she writes in her book, *So Close, I can Feel God's Breath*, "It was amazing, not just to be standing in the midst of such beauty, but to be standing at all. How incredible that I, who could barely walk, could actually summit for the first time in my life!"

The Bible is full of "one another" verses. We are told to love one another, be kind to one another, accept one another, forgive one another, and help one another. Apparently, it matters how we treat each other.

For some, the great draw of hiking is the silence and the solitude. Others prefer having someone to share the sights and sounds and experience with. But even solitary hikers will occasionally encounter others along the way.

Climbing Higher

In Luke 5, the Bible tells the story of a paralyzed man whose friends brought him to Jesus – they removed the roof from a home and dropped him down into the room where Jesus was teaching. Incredibly, Jesus healed him, and he left on his own, carrying his mat! Like the friend of Beverly Rose, we can only imagine how thankful his friends were, that they had made the extra effort to not only transport their friend but found a way to bring him directly into the presence of Jesus.

WISE WORDS: "We are all image bearers of God. How do we reflect Him; how do we make those with disabilities a part of the community?" (Joni E. Tada)

36

Huffy Breaths and Bear Cubs

*Rejoice with those who rejoice;
mourn with those who mourn
(Romans 12:15 NIV)*

Toodles has never been a hiking dog. She is a mix of boxer and hound, and she usually prefers to be pampered at home. I, however, have always wanted a hiking dog. Most of the time, we agree to disagree, and on occasion, we compromise and hit the nearest trail.

One Saturday morning, Toodles and I invited my husband, Andrew, to join us, and we headed for the Ocoee River area in southeast Tennessee. The hike would be about seven miles. For the first two miles, the narrow trail wound through a lush green forest.

Thirty minutes into the hike, Toodles sat down with a firm message of wanting to return to the car. She agreed with a huffy breath to continue but sat down again about every three minutes. I was beyond frustrated. What I hoped would be a soul-cleansing experience in nature turned into more and more huffiness from both Toodles and myself. I gave in.

Andrew would continue the hike by himself for a while, and I would return to the car with Toodles. On the hike back to the car, I wanted to stop every 10 minutes, but Toodles pranced forward almost dragging me back.

When Andrew returned, I could tell something had happened. His face glowed, and his smile stretched wide. Around the very next curve on the trail where Toodles and I turned back, Andrew came upon three bear cubs that played on the trail in front of him. He was able to sit and watch them tumble about. He also noticed their mother just off the trail keeping a parental eye on the man so close to her little cubs.

No one in our family has ever spotted a single bear while hiking, and now he enjoyed four. And I saw none. The mood in the car on the way home was mixed. Andrew was ecstatic. Toodles was happy. And I was crushed with disappointment and anger.

We often are invited to rejoice with those who rejoice and weep with those who weep, but to do both requires a special grace. So often, the experiences of life place us in a position of choosing to enjoy something OR to nurture our pain. In reality, we can do both. It is okay to grieve a loss AND enjoy the visit of our children. We can feel crushed with disappointment AND enjoy the taste of a good meal. There is no guilt in holding hurt AND joy.

On the cross, Jesus experienced pain like no other has ever felt, AND He tenderly cared for His mother, AND with love He saw each of His future children able to be in relationship with God because of His crucifixion.

"Father, help me know that it is okay to hurt and heal, to grieve and laugh, to be disappointed and savor the beauty that is mine."

Story Credit: Wendy C. Brown. Wendy finds God most personal when her feet are on a trail or when sitting amongst the trees.

37

A Perfect Day for Sand Flies

Be alert and of sober mind. (1 Peter 5:8 NIV)

Tennessee taught me much about dangers on the trail. Look for snakes, bears, and most of all mosquitos. Colorado added more. Moose. Snakes with rattles. Elusive mountain lions. Hiking in New Zealand then became a welcome relief. With no natural predators there, I found I could wander mindlessly and for hours without a thought of harm.

Most trails on the South Island are lush rain forests with large palm-like trees that reach skyward to form a canopy of protection from the harsh rays of the sun. Each path seems to whisper a welcome to hikers. *Enjoy. You are safe here.*

On one particular hike, our family spread out on the trail each according to their own style. One pushed forward to reach the end. A couple meandered onward, deep in conversation. I remained behind them all to take pictures of whatever captured my imagination. Wonder filled my soul. Red-capped mushrooms. Ferns. Moisture that rested on leaves close to the ground. I stopped every few minutes to linger with nature and capture its beauty both with my camera and my heart.

The return trip back down the mountain went very much the same. They sauntered off at their own pace, and I breathed in each scent and watched for hidden treasures.

As we neared the van at the end of the trail, we began to sense something ominous. We exited the forest onto a beach area and found that a hoard of sand flies had caught our scent. They swarmed us toward the van. Even with our cries and swift pace, the van filled with the big-toothed monsters. We were several miles down the road before we could escort all of them out of the van. That night we celebrated over dinner together and talked both of the peace of the forest and the dangers that lurked beyond.

Some seasons of life lull us into believing that we have no enemies. They are precious times of relief for which we can be grateful. The Bible teaches us though that we not only have an enemy, but we have one that prowls about like a roaring lion. He is always seeking to destroy us: with lies, disappointment, and negative beliefs about ourselves and God.

Thankfully, we have an armor in just our size. This is no ragtag suit. We have the helmet of salvation to protect us from negative beliefs. Included also is: a breastplate of righteousness to help us make informed choices; the belt of truth to carry other pieces of armor; shoes of peace to lead us through times of discord; the shield of faith for perseverance; and finally, the sword of the Spirit—God's Word—to comfort and strengthen us in battle. All of these tools are ours to use when the enemy intensifies his attack and especially for the moments when he seems to come out of nowhere.

Story Credit: Wendy C. Brown. Wendy is a nature lover, seed planter, writer, and licensed counselor.

38

Waiting For Spring

In the beginning you laid the foundations of the earth. And the heavens are the work of your hands. They will perish, but you remain ... you remain the same. (Psalm 102:25-27 NIV)

One of my most memorable stories from my Appalachian Trail hike involves the weather. It was May 12, and I was seven weeks into my thru hike. It had been cold and wet most of the time, but over the last week or so, the weather turned particularly harsh.

For the past few days, I had been hiking with Rob and Rachel, a couple from Kentucky who came out every year for two weeks to section hike the Appalachian Trail.

"You guys sure did pick the wrong two weeks to come out this year," I told Rob, as we ate breakfast outside of Wise Shelter in the Grayson Highlands of Virginia.

On cue, the cold rain changed to sleet that fell into our last few bites of oatmeal. At that moment, I thought to myself, if it gets much colder today, we're going to see snow. I was becoming even more discouraged than I had been. The weather had beaten me down so far, it had warped my reasoning to the point that I literally thought it would never be warm and sunny over the course of my six-month hike.

I told Rob, "I'm gonna give it to June 1. If the weather doesn't at least show signs of being spring by then, I'm outta here."

"I think you just need a week of good weather to lift your spirits," Rob replied, doing his best to encourage me.

Easy for you to say, I thought. Your hike is finished in just a few days. I'm out here for another four months.

Climbing Higher

The three of us started our daily trek with the sleet continuing. By the time we reached The Scales parking area, big fluffy flakes of snow began to appear as we took a quick break. When we climbed to the top of the 5,000-foot Pine Mountain a mile later, the snow was crunching under our boots on the trail, and we had to stop every 15 minutes or so to brush it from our shoulders. This was a genuine snowstorm ... on May 12!

Rob and Rachel's vehicle was parked in Atkins, Virginia, and they offered to drive me back to Damascus for the annual Trail Days festival. Two days after the snow, we were in a warm vehicle cruising down I-81 at what seemed like unimaginable speed to three weary hikers.

My friend Brian came up that weekend to Damascus to visit me, and I expressed to him my misgivings about the weather and my self-imposed June 1 deadline.

"You just need a week of really good weather," he said, echoing Rob's sentiments and sensing my discouragement, "and according to the extended forecast, I think you're about to get your wish."

Brian was right. The weather finally broke for good on May 19, one week after I got snowed on in the Grayson Highlands. Spring had arrived ... and it was spring for about six days. Then it was summer! My biggest takeaway from hiking the Appalachian Trail is that change happens quickly.

If there is one thing experienced hikers understand, it is not to trust the weather. Rain can become snow, and snow becomes ice. What once seemed safe is now treacherous. A creek that

Waiting For Spring

was once passable, can be quickly changed by a flash flood to a rushing and dangerous current. The heat that seemed bearable, with no breeze and humidity or poor hydration can lead to heat exhaustion or even stroke.

What a blessed discovery to learn there is one unchanging certainty in life. The One who created the limitless wonder of earth, who kindles within us the desire for discovery of it and the appreciation as well, is Himself unchanging. He is always merciful, compassionate, patient, and calling us to come to Him.

Story/Photo Credit: Jason Beck, AT Thru-Hiker, 2021

Climbing Higher

Through Him all things were made (John 1:3)

Photo Credit: Cherokee Hiking Club

39

A Parable of the Saunterer

For since the creation of the world His invisible attributes are clearly seen, being understood by the things that are made (Romans 1:20 NKJV)

The term *saunter* is not widely utilized in modern conversation. Generally, it means to walk in a slow, relaxed manner, without hurry or effort. Author Albert W. Palmer in his 1911 story *The Mountain Trail and Its Message* relates a story he refers to as 'A Parable of Sauntering.' The parable focuses on a life lesson passed on from famed 19th century naturalist John Muir. Palmer's story contains excellent insights even today.

In the parable, Palmer relates being upset upon hearing that Muir did not approve of the word 'hike.' When confronted, Muir responded unequivocally that he liked neither the word nor the thing itself. In his rich Scottish accent Muir challenged his questioner, "People ought to *saunter* in the mountains - not hike."

Muir detailed his objection by providing the origins of the term 'saunter.' He explained that in the Middle Ages when people journeyed to the Holy Land they referred to their destination by the phrase, "A la sainte terre," which translated means "To the Holy Land." And so these pilgrims became known as *sainte-terre-ers*, which became *saunterers*. Referring primarily to the American West, Muir added, "Now these mountains are our Holy Land, and we ought to saunter through them, not merely 'hike' through them."

No one of his generation held the natural world in higher esteem than Muir. His many expeditions across North America, his subsequent writings, and battles for preservation of western lands are clear proof of his love for God's creation. From Muir's perspective the natural world was not even to be traversed in an unworthy manner. The mountains and great outdoors were truly "Holy ground."

Muir's advice rings truer than ever today. One of the greatest benefits of hiking, particularly in today's ultra-connected digital world, is the opportunity to sever ties with the noise and distraction of everyday life. This applies even more so to the Christian. We must quiet our souls to hear God clearly. One of the best ways to do this is to develop our skills as saunterers. The Psalmist proclaims a similar truth, "Be still, and know that I am God." Psalm 46:10 (NKJV).

Regrettably, hikers today seem to value things like pace and mileage over contemplation of the natural world. The trail has become an extension of the gym for many. We bring civilization into nature with earbuds, cellphones, and blaring music. We take to the trail but what are we experiencing? Do we really believe we are on 'Holy ground'?

Believers are able to see, hear and experience more than merely nature. Let us consider the parable and perspective of the saunterer. God's handiwork is a beautiful *destination,* but it can also be an incredibly meaningful part of the *journey.* As we carefully ponder his magnificent creation, God can and does speak into our lives. The trail introduces an incredible world of discovery, introspection, and direction for the believer, but the art of listening must be nurtured. So slow down, wander, calm your mind, soak in the richness of your surroundings. . . and express gratitude. Begin the journey of a saunterer.

Story Credit: Brian A. Boyd is an avid hiker and publisher of multiple hiking and historical guidebooks about North Georgia and the Southern Appalachians.

> HIKING QUOTE: "And into the forest I go, to lose my mind and find my soul." (John Muir)

40
Hikes End

*I have fought the good fight, I have finished the race,
I have kept the faith. (2 Timothy 4:7 NIV)*

I heard the first bird chirp on the last morning of my 1,100 mile thru-hike of the Florida Trail, from the Everglades to the Alabama state line, while leaving the little sparkleberry camp by the river. The path led straight into a fresh burn. Black, dry soot crunched beneath my shoes, and the odor of burnt pine rose strong into the warm, humid morn. No smoke, though.

The Florida Trail popped out at Kennedy Bridge and circled around Hurricane Lake. It was a Saturday morning, and campers were having a ball, fishing, cooking up good smelling breakfasts, kids hollering, all good innocent fun. I crossed the grass-covered earthen dam of the lake and rambled through hills, turning north again, toward Alabama. The hills steepened and clear creeks sliced between them. I pressed on, now excited to see what the end of the Florida Trail looked like. I had visualized all sorts of things – a sign marking the respective Florida-Alabama border, a "You Made It!" banner, or simply the last orange blaze ending at some indefinable boundary of the state forest.

A deer dashed from a ravine, crossing my path. It was just another day for nature's beast, knowing no deadlines and dates, or weekends. This was my last day out with them, and I stood perched on the cusp of such time constraints.

Along the way, I passed an astonishing pitcher plant colony. I had to stop and take a picture, end of the trail or no. Here, hundreds of green "pitchers" were tipped in white over which hung maroon flowers so deeply colored and dense as to be fake. Nature never quits on the Florida Trail. Ahead, the trail dipped,

Climbing Higher

and I could see signage. This was it! I rolled up and sure enough, a kiosk showing the Florida Trail and another trail, heading into Alabama. Here was a register. I signed it, indicating my days of start and finish, and a few other comments. I savored the moment for just a moment, then put my pack on for the last time and began to figure out how to get to the road where my nephew Derek was going to pick me up.

Then, I saw more orange blazes ahead.

I wasn't finished! I hurriedly walked on, tracing the orange markers that I'd been following through the state. They led to a dirt road and the actual Florida-Alabama state line. Appropriately painted onto a pine tree was the last orange blaze. I'd completed the Florida Trail. I raised a fist into the air, then thanked God for giving me the strength to make it happen.

One of the continued refrains of the apostle Paul in the New Testament was of the need to finish well. He wanted it for himself and for those he had discipled and led to faith. He wanted the joy of facing God at heaven's door and hearing the welcome, "well done!" The story is told of the last days of George Jones, the country singer. After days of silence, it is said as he neared death, he looked upward and spoke, "Well hello there. My name is George Jones. I've been looking for you." His wife believed he was speaking to God.

Finishing a hike is certainly a cause for celebration. How much more so to end this life ready to meet God and able to declare "I have finished the greatest race and kept the faith!"

Story Credit: Many thanks to outdoorsman and author, Johnny Molloy, for the contribution of this story.

About the Author

Lettie Kirkpatrick Whisman makes her home in Cleveland, TN where she lives in a 100-year-old historical home on Wildwood Lake. She has written for many inspirational publications. *Climbing Higher Devotion for Hikers* is her fifth book, although her work has also appeared in seven book compilations. She has taught classes for writers at Lifeway Christian Resources, Chattanooga Bible Institute, Kentucky Christian Writers Conference, the Southern Christian Writers Conference and the Southeastern Christian Writers Conference.

Lettie's favorite leisure activity is hiking the nearby East Tennessee and North Georgia mountains with her husband Jim. She is a happy lady when she is discovering a pretty pair of clip-on earrings (!) or sitting outside a café with a book, a Reuben sandwich and a piece of dark chocolate mint. Her most blessed moments are spent enjoying her family, especially the role of "Mimi" to a growing clan of "grand" children.

Additional book purchases and information regarding speaking engagements may be found at her website www.WritingForHim.com.
She may also be contacted through email at
lettiejk@gmail.com
on Facebook at
Lettie Kirkpatrick Whisman
or through correspondence at:
2620 Springplace Road, SE
Cleveland, TN 37323.

Glimpses of Grace: Stories of Hope

. . . offers stories of hope to remind us that God's gracious presence truly penetrates some of life's darkest places.

My husband, Matt, started reading your book and couldn't put it down. Only through the grace of God have you survived. This book touches the heart of human frailties and offers hope to those in need.
Carolyn R. Tomlin

WOW! I'm amazed at the faith path and the grace God has shown you through it all. I'm so glad I got the book!
Edna Pollier

You are an excellent writer and convey the GRACE of our loving Lord which is so abundant and free. You have shown your readers that GOD IS SUFFICIENT!!
Roberta Harper

I just wanted to let you know your book is amazing, it helped me and gave me hope, I finished it in one day. **Donna Dunn Parker**

**For more information
visit www.writingforhim.com
Or email lettiejk@gmail.co**

God's Extravagant Grace for Extraordinary Grief

This I know – our lives can be forever changed in a split second of time . . . the time it takes a stroke to destroy brain cells, a car to crash, a heart to stop. This book is written because God's extravagant grace can redeem even extraordinary grief.

In each trial Lettie has faced, she has chosen to lean into the goodness and sovereignty of God, allowing the Lord to teach her deep truths only learned in deep suffering. **Emily Chadwell**

I wish everyone could have more than this book. I wish every reader could pick up the phone and personally speak with Lettie when they're feeling shaken by suffering. It's what I get to do as her son.
Judson Kirkpatrick

For Lettie Whisman, living by faith in God's extravagant grace is far more than a mere academic perspective. Her life is a testimony of embracing grace.
Jay McCluskey

Lettie has not only walked through "the valley of the shadow of death" but she has camped there. Her writing is real, raw, and thought provoking
Jennifer Mathewson Speer

"As timeless as that mountain seems,
it had a beginning and will have an end.
Its majesty points to a maker
who is bigger and higher and stronger"
        (Deborah P. Brunt)